Trail of the First Wagons
Over the Sierra Nevada

Charles K. Graydon

The Patrice Press
St. Louis, Missouri

Library of Congress Cataloging in Publication Data

Graydon, Charles K., 1908-
     Trail of the First Wagons Over the Sierra Nevada.

    1. Trails — Sierra Nevada Mountains (Calif. and Nev.) — Guide-books. 2. Sierra Nevada Mountains (Calif. and Nev.) — Description and travel — Guide-books. 3. Sierra Nevada Mountains (Calif. and Nev.) — Maps. I. Title.
F868.S5G73   1988   917.94′40453   88-5924
ISBN 0-935284-59-1 (pbk.)

Published by:
The Patrice Press
1701 S. Eighth Street
St. Louis MO 63104

Printed in the United States of America

Dedicated to my two constant, devoted, four-legged trail companions, Amos and Oley. They went all the way.

Amos

Oley

Contents

Foreword

INTERSTATE 80 SLASHES through the foothills and peaks of the Sierra Nevada. Present-day travelers zip past the camping places of the emigrants at a rate of two or three daily camps per hour. When I-80 is closed for a few hours, motorists go home and write indignant letters to the editors of newspapers, complaining that they got cold or hungry while awaiting the snowplows.

All this trouble and inconvenience is just the Sierra's way of reminding the flatlanders of what it might have been like in 1844, in the late fall, when the first snow was falling and exhausted men, women, and kids pulled themselves together to challenge that granite wall and those steep hillsides, brushy canyons, and cold creeks and rivers.

The Sierra Nevada is a huge slab tilted by earth forces so that it has an overall slope from west to east of only a couple of degrees — but an eastern scarp that must have been appalling to the emigrants as they approached the last leg of their 2,000-mile journey to a new land of promise. And beyond those cliffs lay a jumble of hills and canyons.

After the spring mud between the Missouri River and the Rocky Mountains, and the parching summer heat between the Rockies and California, tired men, women, children, and oxen suddenly saw a granite wall standing between them and their new Eden.

Tired but tough, hungry but desperately determined, they crossed that barrier. At first they just went as their experience had taught them — two or three scouts ahead to find what seemed to be the best way, the men and women joining to cut brush or small trees, the youngsters rolling aside the smaller rocks, the animals following to move boulders with chains and sweat — and then the wagons bumping and lurching, sometimes overturning, often breaking a tongue or a wheel.

The next party, and the next, would follow the trace, perhaps varying a little from side to side, cutting out a little more brush, rolling aside a few more rocks, digging out a little more of a hillside that might capsize a wagon. In 1844 the trail didn't exist, but by the time the gold rush started in 1849, it was clearly defined and in use every year until, in the late 1860s, it started to disappear.

Off and on in the years that followed, individuals, history organizations, Boy Scout troops, and governmental agencies sought traces of the trail, which often was called the "Donner Trail," because in the early 1900s the tragedy of the Donner Party was still fresh in the minds of second and third generation Californians.

Thousands of parties survived the ordeal, and it is ironic that the trail became known for a failure. Historians have called it the California Trail, or the Overland Emigrant Trail, or, probably most accurately, the California Portion of the Overland Emigrant Trail. The emigrants themselves had less printable names for it.

Interested parties put up smallish metal or wooden signs here and there, most of which have disappeared. Articles were published in local papers and occasionally in the metropolitan dailies. Mimeographed reports were published in small quantities and filed away. Some diligent searchers returned year after year in their quest. Hikers, horseback parties, snowshoers, and cross-country skiers explored the higher elevations. Their interpretations and conclusions were studied and argued. Often, a new trail addict did not know about the predecessors and "discovered" the remnants of the trail for himself.

Chuck Graydon, retired from the U.S. Armored Cavalry, a mountain man at heart, was one of these "discoverers," admittedly late on the scene. Often alone, sometimes with a friend, always with his dogs, he found himself increasingly impelled to search out the fading marks of a great episode in history. On foot, in a four-wheel-drive truck, on skis — summer and winter, rain, sun — he added bits and pieces to his knowledge and more and more lines on his maps.

After a few years, he became convinced that the bits and pieces should be put together and preserved by some agency that would be available over the years; the logical choice was the U.S. Forest Service, which was glad to cooperate and provide some official sanction for his project as it developed.

Finally, a package was put together of words and maps and turned over to the Tahoe National Forest. A few copies went to friends and those who had helped unofficially, and that lucky few insisted that a wider publication should be done. This book is that result.

— Paul Webster
July 1, 1986

(Paul Webster is author of *The Mighty Sierra* and *Understanding the Sierra Nevada.*)

The Truckee Route in California is now commonly called the "Donner Trail." This title is misleading, since the Donner Party, as such, never completed its journey. Several years ago an attempt was made by civic groups and historical societies to have the state of California change the name "Donner Pass" to "Stephens Pass," in honor of Elisha Stephens, the captain of the first party to to make the transit. In fact, there is a bronze marker at the top of the pass, erected by E Clampus Vitus, proclaiming it as Stephens (Stevens) Pass.

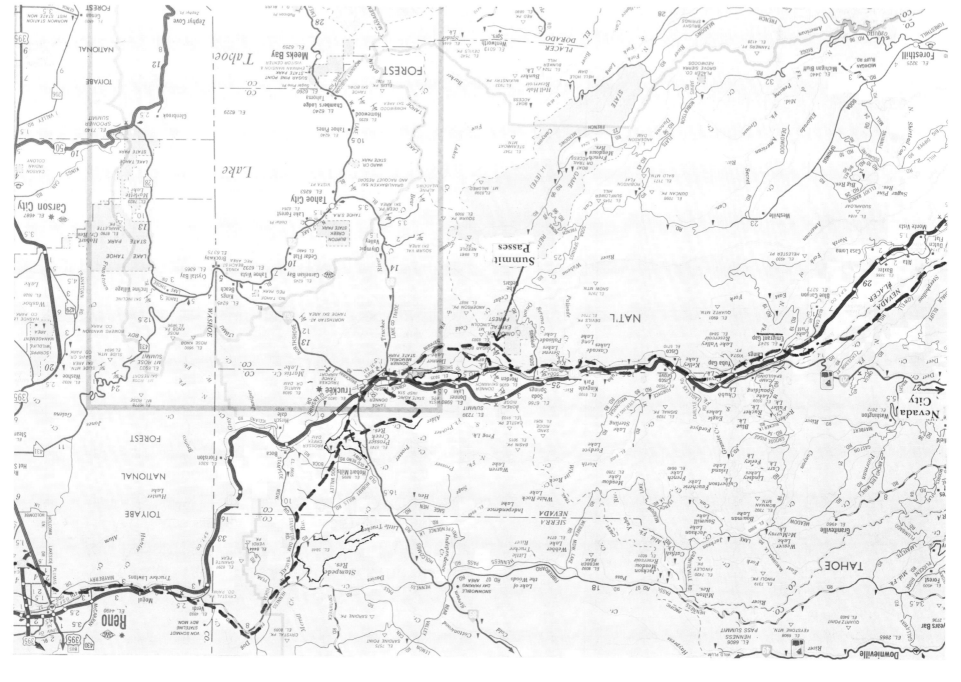

The Truckee Routes
General Trace of the Trail

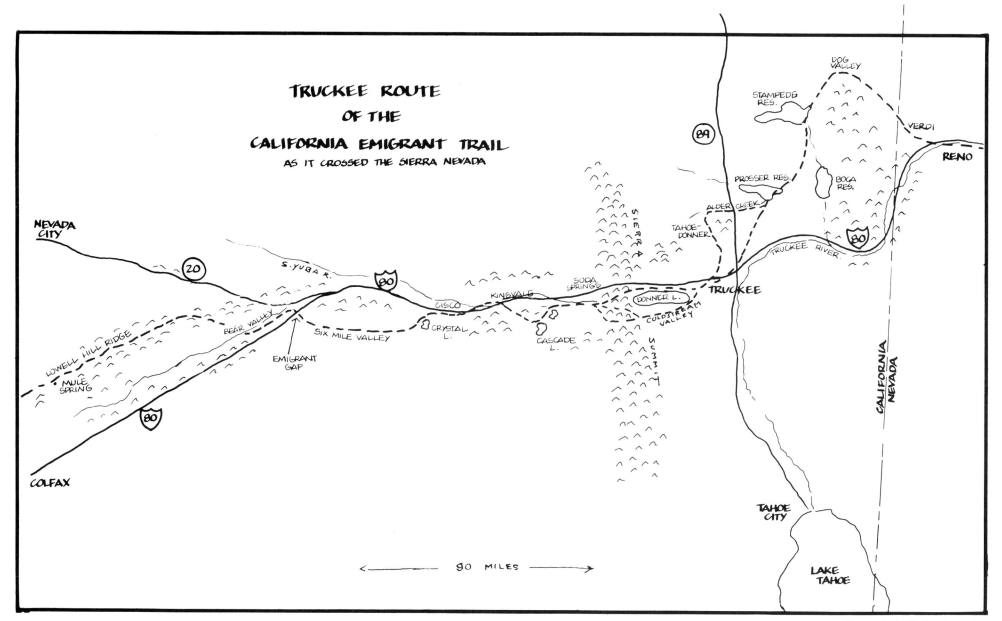

TRUCKEE ROUTE
OF THE
CALIFORNIA EMIGRANT TRAIL
AS IT CROSSED THE SIERRA NEVADA

NEVADA CITY

COLFAX

DOG VALLEY

STAMPEDE RES.

VERDI

RENO

PROSSER RES.

BOCA RES.

ALDER CREEK

TAHOE-DONNER

SIERRA

TRUCKEE RIVER

TRUCKEE

S. YUBA R.

SODA SPRINGS

CISCO

KINGVALE

DONNER L.

COLDSTREAM VALLEY

BEAR VALLEY

SIX MILE VALLEY

CRYSTAL L.

CASCADE L.

SUMMIT

LOWELL HILL RIDGE

MULE SPRING

EMIGRANT GAP

CALIFORNIA NEVADA

TAHOE CITY

LAKE TAHOE

← 90 MILES →

Cartography by Charles K. Graydon

Route of Stevens Party
Council Bluffs, Iowa, to California

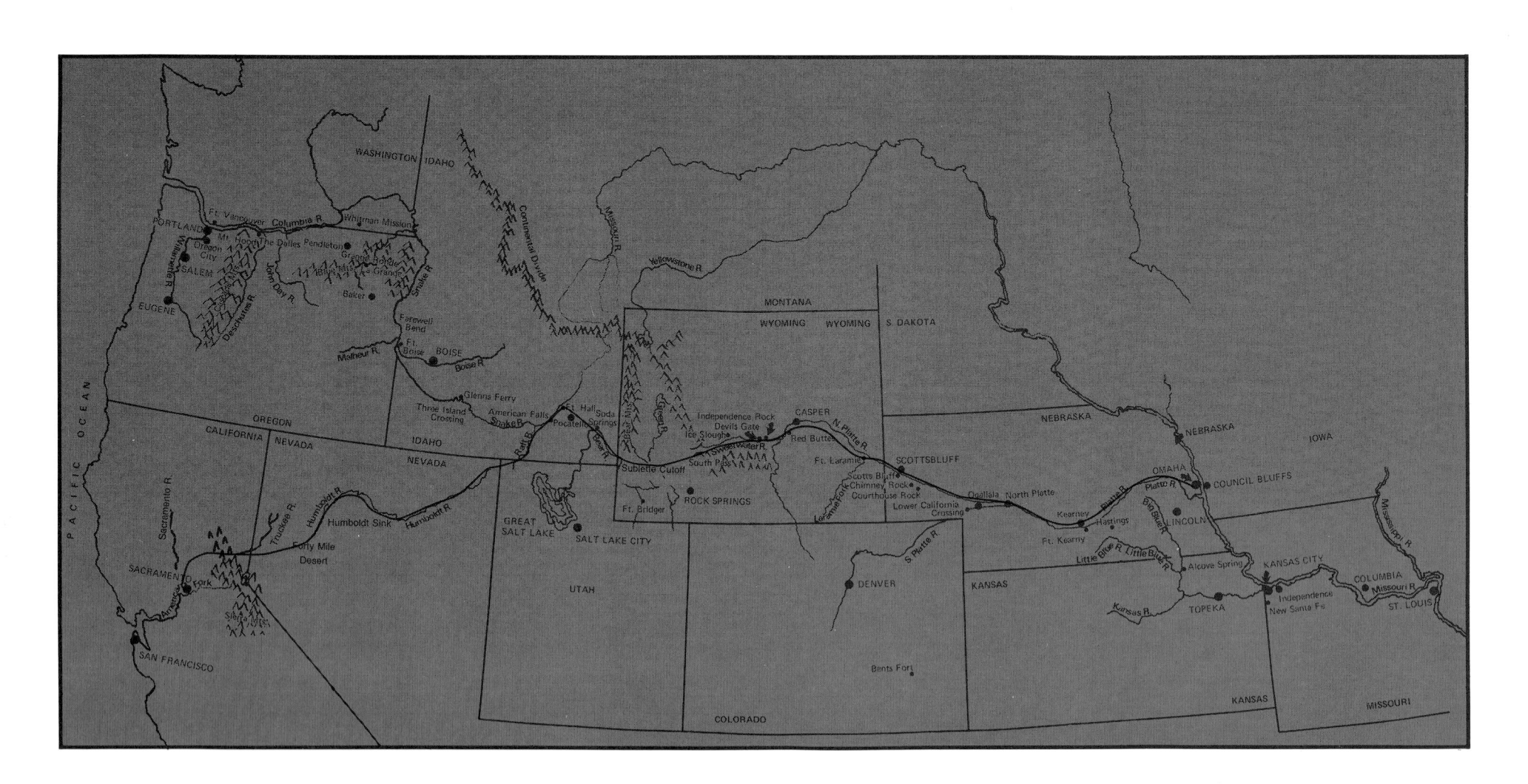

This is the Weddell sign which started the author's interest in mapping the Truckee routes over the High Sierra.

Introduction

IN FEBRUARY 1978, while skiing high up on Mount Judah, I came upon an old weather-beaten sign that read: "Emigrant Trail." My first reaction was: "What on earth were they doing up here?" Less than one-half mile to the north lay famous Donner Pass, over 800 feet below! The answer to this question lay at the end of a six-year search to find out where and how the first emigrants crossed the High Sierra. This search soon became more exciting than a treasure hunt.

At the beginning I was warned to be careful of gold miners, marijuana growers, and other sensitive landowners who might resent seeing a stranger poking around on their property. In actuality, the few owners met were most helpful and glad to have it confirmed that the historic old trail went through their land. These people and dozens of others met along the way said: "You ought to write a book about it," which is the reason for this publication.

It is intended as a guide for those who would like to experience the satisfaction and thrill of treading in the footsteps of those intrepid emigrants who crossed the mighty Sierra Nevada in their quest for better lives. By following even small sections of their route one will learn more than words can tell of the great difficulties these hardy people went through to reach their final destination. From accounts of the emigrants themselves, this was the most difficult section of the route on the long trek from the Missouri River.

The information in this book is taken from my study made for the U.S. Forest Service to record remaining evidence of the Truckee Route of the California Trail through the Tahoe National Forest.

Before embarking on a search for physical evidence of a trail unused for over one hundred and twenty years, its general route had to be established. The emigrant diaries consulted contained only a few accounts detailed enough to determine accurate locations. Fortunately, several people made serious efforts to reidentify sections of the old trail when much more evidence of it still existed. Work by the people and agencies listed in the acknowledgments was particularly useful in establishing the general route of the trail.

It became obvious at the beginning of the fieldwork that little or no evidence of the original trail would be found in areas logged over or altered by road and railroad grading and other works of man. Only in the remaining, little-used remote areas could physical evidence be found. Granite outcrops, rust-stained and worn smooth by the passage of hundreds of iron wagon tires and hubs, provide some of the best positive evidence. In some places the rust has washed off, but the smoothly worn surface of the rock along the trail bed can still be found. In many places the long-unused trail, with little or no plant growth due to the impaction, can still be found. However, in a few instances, trees more than 120 years old stand in the middle of an otherwise impacted trail, proving the wagon road to be at least that old. Rocks which emigrants had set aside on each side of the trail are still there.

Because of the difficulty of traversing wagons across slopes without considerable grading, the trail often went directly up or down slopes that would seem almost impossible to negotiate. These slopes required ''double teaming'' and various methods of winching, braking, and snubbing to ascend or descend. Most of these steep sections now are badly eroded to the point where they look like rocky draws or ditches.

Artifacts remain along the course of the original trail, but time and souvenir hunters have removed most of them. Ox shoes and iron wagon parts were useful in identifying remote sections of the trail.

In many cases it is impossible to state with assurance that the evidence seen was not made by some later traffic. In those sections not restricted by terrain there could have been several routes used to any given point. The location of the most likely original trail evidence is indicated in the detailed trail descriptions and, except where this evidence remains, these descriptions can only indicate the probable trace.

Efforts to preserve the trail through California as a state historical landmark have failed, and soon all signs of it will have gone the way of the emigrants who first blazed it. Man has joined nature in its final obliteration. Last year the area around historic Mule Spring was logged out again and signs of the old trail no longer exist there. The beautiful, large cedars along the trail on the south side of Negro Jack Hill are marked for cutting. Almost two miles of the trail in Cold Stream Valley are being wiped out by an ongoing gravel operation. A ski resort had been planned for this valley and on the pristine east slope of Mount Judah above it, where the old trail leads to the two high passes over the Sierra summit. As this is written, another section of the trail has just been wiped out in Six Mile Valley for another ski resort.

There is, however, a bright spot on the horizon. The Oregon-California Trails Association (OCTA) caused a bill to be passed in August 1984 to include the California Trail in the National Historic Trails Act. This will provide for identification, interpretation, and protection of the trail on all federal land and encourage its preservation on all other land. If this measure is not implemented very soon there will be little left of this great historical treasure.

The Truckee-Donner Historical Society also was instrumental in arresting damage proposed for the trail by the developers of the ski resort in Cold Stream Valley.

Well over one mile of once-beautiful Cold Stream Valley has been turned into a vast gravel pit.

Acknowledgments

PETER M. WEDDELL of San Jose spent most of his summers from 1920 to 1952 marking the trail from Verdi, Nevada, to the Sierra summit. Only a few of his fast-deteriorating wooden signs still remain. Dr. Earl Rhoads worked closely with Weddell and left many white, triangular blazes along the trail. Clyde Arbuckle, Western historian, also of San Jose, who accompanied Weddell on much of his research, was most helpful in providing details of their findings, including a map made by Rhoads.

Wendell Robie of Auburn and his ''Mountain Lions'' undertook to mark the trail beginning at Donner Lake in 1934. His trail descriptions and few remaining metal signs were useful in helping to locate the trail between Summit Valley and Mule Springs. He was most helpful in lending his assistance.

In 1949 the Department of Beaches and Parks, State of California, made a study to develop the trail as a state historical monument beginning at Donner Lake. Their report contains a trail description, map, and excellent summary of emigrant diaries. Unfortunately, the state did not fund this project.

Bert Wiley of Sacramento has devoted many years to trail research. His book was distributed in November 1982 after most of the field work for this survey was finished. It was useful in corroborating work already done and providing additional clues.

In 1974 the Nevada Emigrant Trail Marking Committee

(NETMC) of the Nevada Historical Society placed solid steel markers at eight key points along the trail in California as far as Donner Summit. These markers are still in place.

Maps from a General Land Office survey in 1864-66 spotted the Emigrant Trail as it crossed section boundaries from Cold Stream Valley to Summit Valley, from Crystal Lake to Carpenter Flat, and on Lowell Hill Ridge.

Pen Pictures from the Garden of the World, edited by H. S. Foote in 1888, contains the story of the Stevens-Townsend-Murphy Party, said to be taken from notes dictated by Moses Schallenberger to his daughter Maggie. Much of the history of this party herein is condensed and, in some cases quoted, from Schallenberger's story.

Foresters and staff members of the Tahoe National Forest lent invaluable assistance to this project in every way possible.

Harold Curran of Reno and Paul Webster of Auburn helped the writer locate sections of the trail near Truckee and Six Mile Valley respectively. Also, many local people met along the way helped piece together bits of knowledge as to where the old trail crossed the Sierra.

— Charles K. Graydon
August 1986

The Truckee Route of the California Trail

THE TAHOE NATIONAL FOREST straddles the Sierra Nevada for seventy miles beginning near California's eastern border. Here, the Truckee route of the California Emigrant Trail passed over some of the most rugged country found on any of the western trails. The eastern approaches to the summit are defended by awesome granite escarpments, steep, heavily wooded slopes, and precipitous rock slides. The western slopes are characterized by a seemingly endless series of narrow ridges, deep canyons, and boulder-strewn streambeds.

In July 1849 a Mr. Badman with the Virginia-Charleston Mining Company party described this area well in his diary: "... seventeen miles over the damndest mountains I ever seen or hird of for wagons to be drove over." T. H. Jefferson, on his map sold as a trail guide in 1849, included a more formal description: "The western descent of these mountains is the most rugged and difficult part of the whole journey [from Independence]."

How the first emigrants conquered the Sierra Nevada is a dramatic story.

In 1840 Americans had settled only as far west as the Missouri River, but by then the country was beginning to fill up and people were thinking of moving west again. A few Americans had come to Mexican-governed California and, as stories of the good lands in Oregon and California began to filter back, the great tide of migration began. The first sizeable emigrant wagon trains arrived in Oregon in 1843 and the following year the Stevens-Townsend-Murphy party brought the first wagons over the Sierra Nevada into the Sacramento Valley by what became known as the Truckee Route.

Two previous attempts had been made to bring wagons over the Sierra. In 1841 the Bartelson-Bidwell party, after getting lost in the desert country of eastern Nevada, abandoned their wagons near Pequop Summit because of loss of oxen. They crossed the Sierra on foot and horseback at or near the present Sonora Pass. In 1843 the Chiles-Walker party got their wagons as far as the Owens Valley on the eastern side of the Sierra. Here they went south on horseback and crossed the summit by way of the present Walker Pass.

The Stevens party left Council Bluffs, Iowa, in the spring of 1844 and crossed the Sierra summit in November of that year. The party consisted of twenty-three men, eight women (two of whom were pregnant), fifteen children and eleven wagons. Elisha Stevens, a former trapper and blacksmith, was elected wagonmaster, and Caleb Greenwood, an old mountain man, was hired on as guide. Greenwood brought with him his two sons by a Crow Indian woman.

The family of Martin Murphy, an immigrant from Ireland by way of Canada and the Missouri Valley, comprised twenty-two members of the party. It was fortunate in having a doctor with it — Dr. John Townsend. With him were his wife and brother-in-law, seventeen-year-old Moses Schallenberger. As later events proved, this was one of the best-led and organized parties to make the crossing into California.

This wagon train followed the recently opened Oregon Trail across Nebraska and southern Wyoming to Fort Hall, Idaho, a Hudson's Bay Company trading post, arriving there the middle of August. In order to get to California the party soon had to leave the Oregon Trail. On trappers' advice and "flying blind," they elected to turn south off the trail at the Raft River and thence into northeastern Nevada. Some say that they may have followed tracks left by the three wagons of the Chiles-Walker party the year before.

The party soon came to Mary's River (now the Humboldt) in the vicinity of present Wells and followed it across Nevada generally along today's I-80. Arriving at the Humboldt Sink, where the river gradually disappears into the ground (about seventy miles east of present Reno), they were uncertain as to what course to take.

Fortunately they met a friendly Paiute Indian and this meeting may have meant the difference between the success and failure of

Elisha Stevens, captain of the Stevens-Townsend-Murphy party

their trip to California. This important event is best described in Moses Schallenberger's story:

> The party seemed to have plenty of previsions, and the only doubtful question was the route they should pursue. A desert lay before them, and it was necessary that they should make no mistake in the choice of a route. Old Mr. Greenwood's contract as pilot had expired when they reached the Rocky Mountains. Beyond that he did not pretend to know anything. Many anxious consultations were held, some contending that they should go due west. Finally, an old Indian was found, called Truckee, with whom old man Green talked by means of signs and diagrams drawn on the ground. From him it was learned that fifty or sixty miles to the west there was a river that flowed easterly from the mountains, and that along this stream there were large trees and good grass. Acting on this information, Dr. Townsend, Captain Stevens, and Joseph Foster, taking Truckee as a guide, started out to explore this route, and after three days returned, reporting that they had found the river just as the Indian had described it. Although there was still a doubt in the minds of some as to whether this was the proper route to take, none held back when the time came to start. In fact, there was no time for further discussion.

After crossing the notorious Forty-mile Desert, where many emigrants and thousands of livestock later died, the party reached the Truckee River near the present town of Wadsworth, Nevada. Following the river, they entered the tortuous upper Truckee canyon near the present California border.

Schallenberger's story vividly describes the struggle up this canyon:

> Then commenced the ever-to-be remembered journey up the Truckee to the summit of the Sierras. At first it was not discouraging. There was plenty of wood, water, grass, and game, and the weather was pleasant. The oxen were well rested, and for a few days good progress was made. Then the hills began to grow nearer together, and the country was so rough and broken that they frequently had to travel in the bed of the stream. The river was so crooked that one day they crossed it ten times in traveling a mile. This almost constant traveling in the water softened the hoofs of the oxen, while the rough stones in the bed of the river worn them down, until the cattle's feet were so sore that it became torture for them to travel. The whole party were greatly fatigued by the incessant labor. But they dared not rest. It was near the middle of October, and a few light snows had already fallen,

The Stevens party often used the river as a trail in the Upper Truckee Canyon.

warning them of the imminent danger of being buried in the snow in the mountains. They pushed on, the route each day becoming more and more difficult. Each day the hills seemed to come nearer together and the stream to become more crooked.

They were now compelled to travel altogether in the bed of the river, there not being room between its margin and the hills to furnish foothold to an ox. The feet of the cattle became so sore that the drivers were compelled to walk beside them in the water, or they could not be urged to take a step; and, in many instances, the teams had to be trebled in order to drag the wagons at all. On top of all those disheartening conditions came a fall of snow a foot deep, burying the grass from the reach of the cattle, and threatening them with starvation. The poor, foot-sore oxen, after toiling all day, would stand and bawl for food all night, in so piteous a manner that the emigrants would forget their own misery in their pity for their cattle. But there was nothing to offer them except a few pine leaves, which were of no effect in appeasing their hunger. Still the party toiled on, hoping soon to pass the summit and reach the plains beyond, and that beautiful land so eloquently described to them by Father Hookins. In face of all these obstacles, there was no thought of turning back. One day they came to some rushes that were too tall to be entirely covered by the snow; the cattle ate these so greedily that two of James Murphy's oxen died. However, by constant care in regulating the amount of this food, no evil effects were experienced, although it was not very nourishing. These rushes were scattered at irregular intervals along the river, and scouts were sent out each day to find them and locate a camp for the night.

The party arrived near the present town of Truckee on November 14. Because of the awesome granite escarpment that lay before them they detached a party of four men and two women to travel by horseback south toward present Lake Tahoe in an attempt to find an alternate route to get to Captain John Sutter's fort in the Sacramento Valley and bring back supplies.

Here, Schallenberger's story best describes the historic first crossing of the Sierra summit:

The party with the wagons proceeded up the tributary, or Little Truckee [now Donner Creek], a distance of two miles and a half, when they came to the lake since known as Donner Lake. They now had but one mountain between them and California, but this seemed an impassable barrier. Several days were spent in attempts to find a pass, and finally the route, over which the present railroad is, was selected. The oxen were so worn out that some of

This is the vertical rock in Donner Pass described by Moses Schallenberger.

the party abandoned the attempt to get their wagons any further. Others determined to make another effort. Those who determined to bring their wagons were Martin Murphy, Jr., James Murphy, James Miller, Mr. Hitchcock, and old Mr. Martin, Mrs. James Murphy's father. The others left their wagons.

The snow on the mountains was now about two feet deep. Keeping their course on the north side of the lake until they reached its head, they started up the mountain. All the wagons were unloaded and the contents carried up the hill. Then the teams were doubled and the empty wagons were hauled up. When about half way up the mountain they came to a vertical rock about ten feet high. It seemed now that everything would have to be abandoned except what the men could carry on their backs. After the tedious search they found a rift in the rock, just about wide enough to allow one ox to pass at a time. Removing the yokes from the cattle, they managed to get them one by one through this chasm to the top of the rock. There the yokes were replaced, chains were fastened to the tongues of the wagons, and carried to the top of the rock, where the cattle were hitched to them. Then the men lifted the wagons, while the cattle pulled at the chains, and by this ingenious device the vehicles were all, one by one, got across the barrier.

They crossed the summit on November 25. Three young men, Joseph Walker, Allen Montgomery, and Moses Schallenberger, had remained at Donner Lake to guard the six wagons left there. They built a cabin but soon departed because heavy snows prevented them from finding enough game to survive the winter. One, Schallenberger, reached the top of the pass but had to return to the lake because of illness. There he spent the winter alone, living on foxes which he trapped. His winter ordeal is a story in itself.

In the meanwhile, with no trail to follow, the main party began the western descent and in about three days arrived near present Big Bend on the South Yuba River. Because of further loss of oxen, heavy snows, and starvation conditions, the men built a cabin where they left the women, children, and wagons, and fought their way to Sutter's Fort in the Sacramento Valley for supplies and assistance. They arrived in early December and were joined there by the party on horseback that had left them near Donner Lake.

Their troubles were not over. It is not clear whether they volunteered or were coerced by the Mexican governor of California to fight against a revolution then going on. It is known that the revolutionists were unfriendly to Americans, so the men may have gone to fight in their own interests. The fighting led them as far

Donner Lake can be seen looking east from Donner Pass. Because of ill-ness, Moses Schallenberger turned back to the cabin at the east end of the lake.

Donner Pass would have looked even more formidable to the ill-fated emigrants of 1846, for then it was shrouded in a deep blanket of snow.

south as Santa Barbara; consequently, it was not until February 1845 that they got back to bring their families and Moses Schallenberger out of the mountains. It was not until June that they could return with oxen to Big Bend and Donner Lake and bring the first wagons over the Sierra into the Sacramento Valley. Unlike most of those who followed, this wagon party arrived in California with more people than it started out with — there were two births along the way and no deaths.

With only two major deviations, the route the Stevens-Townsend-Murphy party pioneered across the Sierra was to become the route followed by thousands of emigrants and gold seekers thereafter.

In early spring of 1845 Caleb Greenwood, traveling east with his two sons, sought a way to avoid the rugged upper Truckee Canyon. From Donner Lake he made a long detour to the northeast to Dog Valley and thence southeast to the Truckee below the canyon.

In the fall of 1845 Greenwood, guiding the Thomas Knight party, avoided upper Truckee Canyon by taking this route from east to west and turning off the river near present Verdi, Nevada. He followed a ravine northwest to Dog Valley and from there southwest down through the present Stampede and Prosser reservoir areas to Donner Lake. Thereafter, this bypass became the main trail to the lake.

The pass opened by the Stevens party (Donner Pass) was used by those who followed until late September 1846, when the Joseph Aram party scouted out a route to avoid the steep wall of Donner Pass. They found a route up Cold Stream Valley to a saddle 7,850 feet high between Mounts Judah and Lincoln, less than two miles south of the original pass. This pass was relatively easy to approach until the last 400 feet, where it rises precipitously up a thirty-degree slope.

Several days behind the Aram party, a group captained by Nicholas Carriger and guided by Greenwood reached the pass.* In order to reach the summit, Carriger's diary indicates that they led twelve yoke of oxen to the top, let down long chains and pulled one wagon at a time to the top. A log roller, laid across the lip of the pass over which the chains were passed, served to lessen the friction. This pass soon became known as ''Roller Pass.'' It was

---

*Some historians credit Carriger's party as being the first to pioneer this pass.

The route opened in 1845 by the Thomas Knight party dropped down a steep slide into Dog Valley, which became a watering and resting place along the trail.

The trail opened by the Aram party in 1846 entered Cold Stream Valley one-half mile south of Donner Lake.

Western descent of the Truckee Route as seen by the Stevens party after it crossed the summit passes

The awesome lip of Roller Pass

Cold Stream Pass (in center of photo) between Mount Judah and Donner Peak

Graydon rests high above Donner Lake at the meadows on the east side of Mount Judah.

perhaps two years later that a large party cut a switchback trail up the unbelievably steep mountainside.

Soon after Roller Pass was opened an easier pass was located between Donner Pass and Mount Judah, sometimes called Middle or Cold Stream Pass. Although both of these passes are over 800 feet higher than Donner Pass, they were easier to approach. Therefore, they soon carried the bulk of the traffic on the Truckee Route until toll roads were built across Donner Pass. The Dutch Flat-Donner Lake Wagon Road, built in 1864 by the Central Pacific Railroad, was the best of those roads.

The three trails over the summit converged at Summit Valley near present Norden, and from there to the Sierra foothills the entire route became a constant fight to overcome a myriad of steep ridges and valleys, rock-strewn canyons, and granite outcroppings.

Issac Wistar, an 1849 gold seeker, described Summit Valley and the western descent of the mountains from the top of Donner Peak as follows:

> While the mules were resting and being readjusted in the pass, I undertook to reach the summit of a high (not the highest) peak on the right, in which there was no great difficulty till near the top, where it was necessary to "coon it" on hands and knees up the sharp corner of a mass of naked rock clear of snow. It was bitterly cold, but from the almost pointed summit, the grandeur and wild, confused desolation of the prospect was sublime indeed. North, east and south, peak rose beyond peak in endless succession while in the west the eye looked far down into a chasm where every ravine and gorge shone and glistened with the spotless white of vast snowfields, and beyond, instead of the expected Sacramento Valley, nothing broke the magnificent expanse of the mountain chains. Thousands of feet down in the chasm but by no means at the bottom shone an emerald valley of brightest green surrounded with snowfields and intersected by a lovely stream, sparkling from afar on its way through these fastnesses to the golden Sacramento. Probably no human foot had ever before rested on the spot where I stood, but the wind roared and howled, the day was drawing to a close, and, nearly frozen, I hastened down to mark out the beautiful valley below for camp, where I found the train had nearly arrived, but had unfortunately stopped short of it in a worse place.

From Summit Valley the trail passed left through a low gap and proceeded west through the Kilborn, Kidd, and Cascade Lakes area. At the west end of the lakes it dropped down to the valley of

These stumps remained from woodcutting efforts of the Donner family at Alder Creek. Now rotted away, they provided evidence for more than a century of the fearsome depth of the snow during the winter of 1846-47.

George Donner built his lean-to against a large pine in the winter of 1846-47. The tree, at right, still lives.

the South Yuba River in the vicinity of Kingvale.

Many emigrant journals reported that the section down the South Yuba was perhaps the roughest trail yet encountered. In 1859 Cyrus Loveland wrote this: ''For me to attempt a description of the road today is useless for I do not believe language can do it. If wagons had never traveled it I would have said it was impossible. It beats anything we have seen on the route for rocks.''

At a point northwest of Cisco Butte the trail turned south up a ridge. After passing Crystal Lake, it continued south up to a saddle where it dropped down into Six Mile Valley. Here it continued north of the North Fork of the American River into Carpenter Flat and thence over Emigrant Gap into Bear Valley. The old trail then went southeast down Bear Valley before turning west up to the top of Lowell Hill Ridge. It followed the top of the ridge to Camel's Hump, at the western boundary of the Tahoe National Forest, continued through present day Chicago Park and ultimately reached Johnson's Ranch near Wheatland in the Sacramento Valley.

Only the Stevens party used the Truckee Route in 1844. In 1845 about fifty wagons made the crossing, and in 1846 it is estimated that close to 500 wagons crossed. In 1849, the first year of the gold rush, the trail was crowded by several thousand wagons.

The Donner Party created the most dramatic and publicized episode in the history of the western trails of America. Following the Truckee Route far behind the other emigrants in 1846, they reached the foot of the summit range late in October and became snowbound. George and Jacob Donner and their families had pulled off the trail near the mouth of Alder Creek because of a broken wagon, while the main party continued on to Donner Lake seven miles distant. Of the eighty-six people at these two camps, only one-half were brought out of the mountains alive, rescued by four relief parties and one small party of their own.

In 1847 Gen. Stephen W. Kearny was eastward bound after participating in the American conquest of California. Sgt. Nathaniel Jones, a member of Kearny's column, painted a vivid picture of the Donner camps as they appeared several months after the tragedy:

June 22: — We came down the lake to some cabins that had been built by some of the immigrants last fall. They were overtaken in the snow. There were eighty of them in number, and only thirty of them that lived. The rest of them starved to death. The General called a halt and detailed five men to bury the deserted bodies of the others. One man lived about four months on human flesh. He sawed their heads open, ate their brains and mangled up their bodies in a horrible manner. This place now goes by the name of Cannibal Camp. While we were stopped here the men came up with our pack mules. Col. Fremont passed us here, the first time we have seen him since we left Fort Sutter. After we had buried the bones of the dead, which were sawed and broken to pieces for the marrow, we set fire to the cabin. One mile above here there was another cabin and more dead bodies but the General did not order them buried.

In 1848 the Carson Route of the California Trail was opened, crossing the Sierra at present Carson Pass, as well as the Lassen Route, which crossed near the Oregon border. These two roads soon drew off most of the traffic from the more difficult Truckee Route.

It is a tribute to the trail judgment of Elisha Stevens and his party that the Central Pacific Railroad, the Liberty Highway, U.S. Highway 40, and finally I-80 all cross the Sierra close to the route they pioneered. It is ironic that the name Stevens soon went down into oblivion, while the pass that he opened is known only as Donner Pass, named after a party that never made it. It is interesting to note, however, that at the top of the same pass is a bronze plaque proclaiming it as "Stephens [Stevens] Pass." Local historical organizations failed in an attempt to have this name change made several years ago.

The Public Land System
of the United States

Township grid references were used in the original trail survey to identify certain map locations, and some are included in this document. For those unfamiliar with this system, the following trail descriptions, when used in conjunction with the maps, should suffice to locate the trail on the ground without reference to the grid references. The maps reproduced herein are taken from U.S. Geodetic Survey (USGS) topographic maps, 7.5 minute series.

Each state in the United States is divided into townships, six miles east and west and six miles north and south. The townships are numbered east or west of principal meridians of longitude, and north or south of parallels of latitude.

Each of the numbered one-mile squares within a township is

called a section, and for purposes of legal description each of the sections is referred to as N½, S½, E½, or W½. The usual division, though, is the quarter-section: SE¼, NE¼, SW¼, or NW¼. Each of those quarters is further divided into sixteenth- sections, indicated as NE¼ of the SW¼, or SE¼ of the SW¼, for examples. Those divisions measure 440 yards on a side.

The maps on the following pages are slightly reduced from the actual size of the USGS quads, which are produced on a scale of 2⅝": 1 mile.

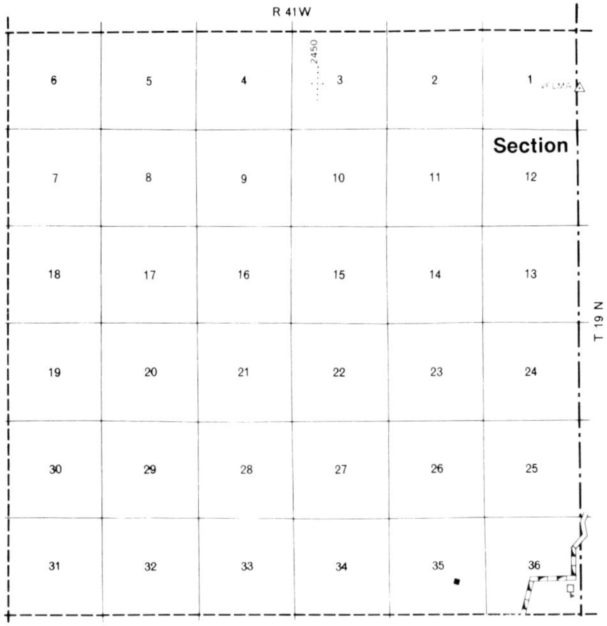

Township

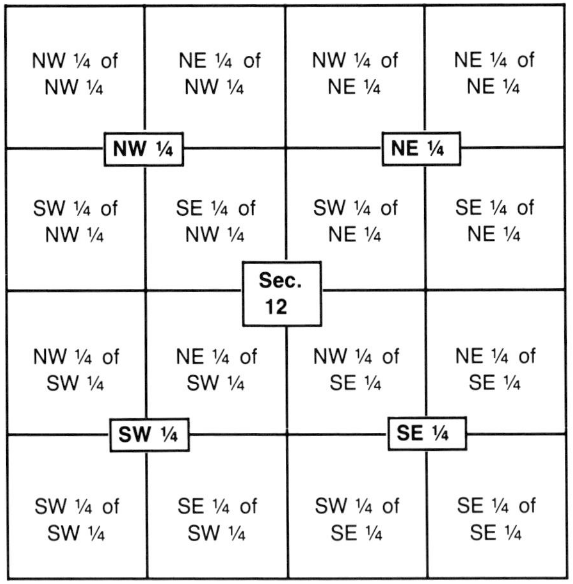

Section

Key to the Maps

Primary highway, hard surface ....

Secondary highway, hard surface ....

Light-duty road, hard or improved surface ....

Unimproved road ....

Trail ....

Railroad: single track ....

Railroad: multiple track ....

Bridge ....

Drawbridge ....

Tunnel ....

Footbridge ....

Overpass—Underpass ....

Power transmission line with located tower ....

Landmark line (labeled as to type) .... TELEPHONE

Dam with lock ....

Canal with lock ....

Large dam ....

Small dam: masonry — earth ....

Buildings (dwelling, place of employment, etc.) ....

School—Church—Cemeteries .... Cem

Buildings (barn, warehouse, etc.) ....

Tanks; oil, water, etc. (labeled only if water) .... • • • Water Tank

Wells other than water (labeled as to type) .... o Oil   o Gas

U.S. mineral or location monument — Prospect .... ▲   x

Quarry — Gravel pit .... ⊗   x

Mine shaft—Tunnel or cave entrance .... ▫   Y

Campsite — Picnic area .... ⚑   ⚞

Located or landmark object—Windmill .... o   ⚙

Rock: bare or awash .... ★   ✳

Horizontal control station .... △

Vertical control station .... BM×671   ×672

Road fork — Section corner with elevation .... ⟋429   + 58

Checked spot elevation ....   × 5970

Unchecked spot elevation ....   × 5970

Boundary: national ....

State ....

county, parish, municipio ....

civil township, precinct, town, barrio ....

incorporated city, village, town, hamlet ....

reservation, national or state ....

small park, cemetery, airport, etc. ....

land grant ....

Township or range line, U.S. land survey ....

Section line, U.S. land survey ....

Township line, not U.S. land survey ....

Section line, not U.S. land survey ....

Fence line or field line ....

Section corner: found—indicated .... +   +

Boundary monument: land grant—other .... ▫   ▫

Index contour .... Intermediate contour ...

Supplementary cont. .... Depression contours ...

Cut — Fill .... Levee

Mine dump .... Large wash

Dune area .... Tailings pond

Sand area .... Distorted surface

Tailings .... Gravel beach

Glacier .... Intermittent streams

Perennial streams .... Aqueduct tunnel

Water well—Spring .... Falls

Rapids .... Intermittent lake

Channel .... Small wash

Sounding—Depth curve ..10 .... Marsh (swamp)

Dry lake bed .... Land subject to controlled inundation

Woodland .... Mangrove

Submerged marsh .... Scrub

Orchard .... Wooded marsh

Vineyard .... Bldg. omission area

Notes For
Trail Explorers

THE DONNER PASS region of the Sierra Nevada is subject to some of the heaviest snowfalls in the country. It is not unusual for the snow to reach depths of twenty to thirty feet on and near the summit. Except on blown-out roads, skis, snowshoes, and snowmobiles are needed, sometimes beginning in late November through early May. (Remember, the Donner Party became completely snowbound 1000 feet below the summit in late October 1846). It's best to check local highway departments for road conditions during winter months.

Temperatures throughout the year are fairly moderate for mountain country, although it can get very hot in the summer below the 5000-foot level. Trail buffs will find spring and fall the most comfortable time to do their exploring. Avid backcountry skiers can get a real thrill experiencing the problems of those emigrants who came late in the season and had to make the winter crossing. The old trail is never more than two or three miles from good county and forest service roads found on both sides of I-80. From these, some parts of the trail can be reached with 4x4 vehicles, but most require good footwork and rock scrambling.

Detailed Maps
and Trail Descriptions

Sections of USGS topographic maps have been reproduced throughout this book in order to facilitate location of the trail. The wagon roads were mapped out and then printed onto these maps in red.

To ensure that the trail's route is correctly represented, each map includes the printer's registration marks. If any marks are out of register, note the difference between the red and black marks and compensate by mentally shifting the trail by the same distance.

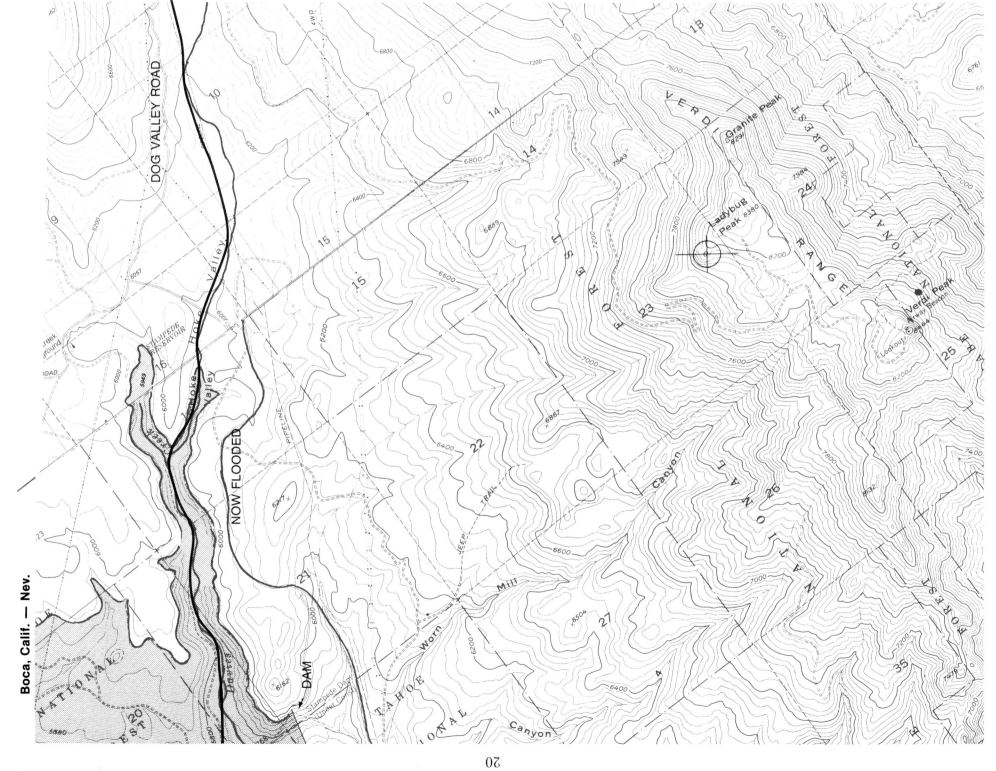

Boca, Calif. — Nev.

DOG VALLEY ROAD

STAMPEDE RESERVOIR

NOW FLOODED

DAM

Stampede Dam Under Const.

Granite Peak

Ladybug Peak 8380

Verdi Peak

VERDI RANGE

NATIONAL FOREST

TAHOE NATIONAL FOREST

Canyon

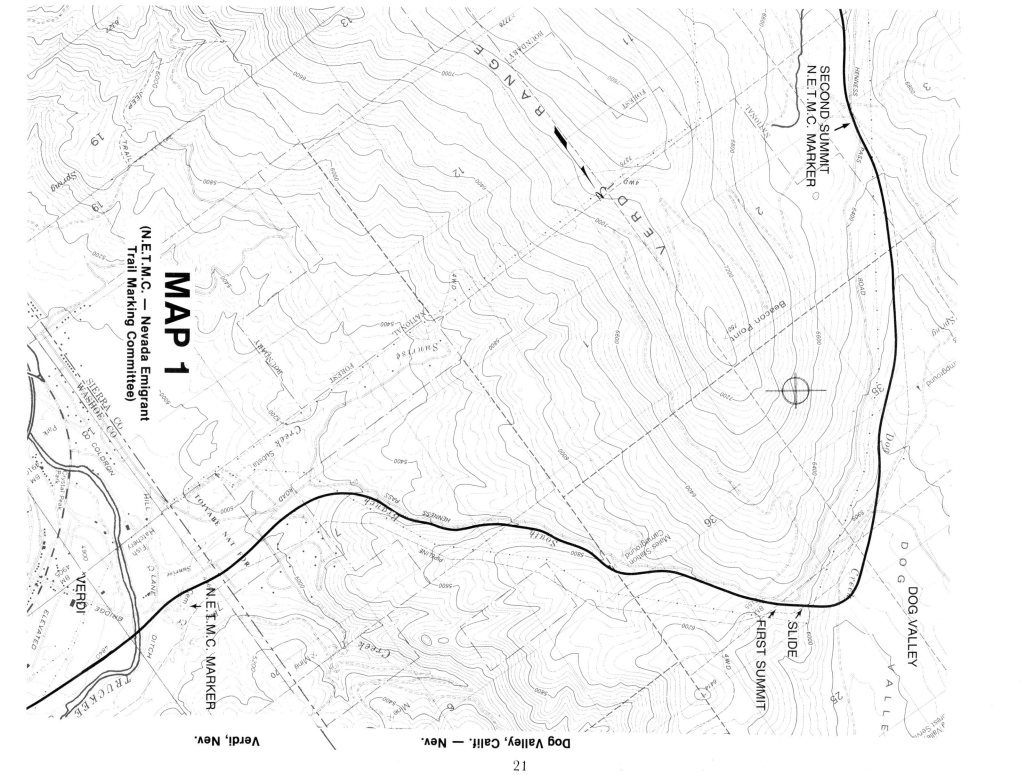

MAP 1

(N.E.T.M.C. — Nevada Emigrant
Trail Marking Committee)

SECOND SUMMIT
N.E.T.M.C. MARKER

N.E.T.M.C. MARKER

Verdi, Nev.

Dog Valley, Calif. — Nev.

FIRST SUMMIT

SLIDE

DOG VALLEY

Map 1   Verdi, Nevada, to Stampede Reservoir

THE TRUCKEE ROUTE of the California Trail entered California about one mile northwest of Verdi, Nevada. It then proceeded northwest up the steep, narrow valley of the South Branch of Dog Creek to Dog Valley. The beginning of this ascent is marked by a Nevada Emigrant Trail Marking Committee (NETMC) marker 100 yards north of the old Crystal Peak Cemetery on the Dog Valley Road one mile northwest of Verdi. The Dog Valley Road is also referred to as Henness Pass Road or Old Reno Road. The present road is graded up the west side of the valley; however, the original trail kept on or close to the dry creek bed to avoid the steep slope. Fill from the road grading has made the creek bed much narrower than it originally was, and several floods have completely altered it.

Approximately two miles northwest, the valley widens around a spring at the USFS Mole's Station campground, now abandoned, where another NETMC sign marks the trail. Here, along the east side of the drainage, can be seen what appears to be the impaction of covered wagons. About one mile farther up, the trail crested at "First Summit" and then dropped down a steep slide into beautiful Dog Valley. A shallow, eroded slide covered by thick underbrush in direct extension of the northwest course of the Henness Pass Road marks the drop into the valley. In 1849 Wakeman Bryarly wrote of the ascent up South Branch, describing Dog Valley as follows:

"We opened upon a beautiful little valley with a very steep hill to descend to it. We went down in the valley and nooned. This valley is oval in shape and had plenty of good grass and water in it."

The trail turned southwest out of Dog Valley on an easy two-mile pull up a draw parallel to and below the Henness Pass Road until it reached "Second Summit," where there is another NETMC marker and a Tahoe National Forest entrance sign. Looking southwest from here the emigrants had their first view of the awesome Sierra summit, and from there the trail proceeded down the center of Hoke Valley. The wide, pipeline grading coming up out of Dog Valley and heading down Hoke Valley has obliterated signs of the old trail except in one short stretch one-third mile southwest of Second Summit, where the telltale rust-marked granite rocks can still be seen.

The trail led to the foot of Hoke Valley, where flooding caused by Stampede Reservoir prevents tracing the trail on the ground. Evidence found by Peter Weddell and Clyde Arbuckle established the route shown on the map, of the trail down Davies Creek.

This Nevada Emigrant Trail Marking Committee marker is at Mole's Station campground above Verdi.

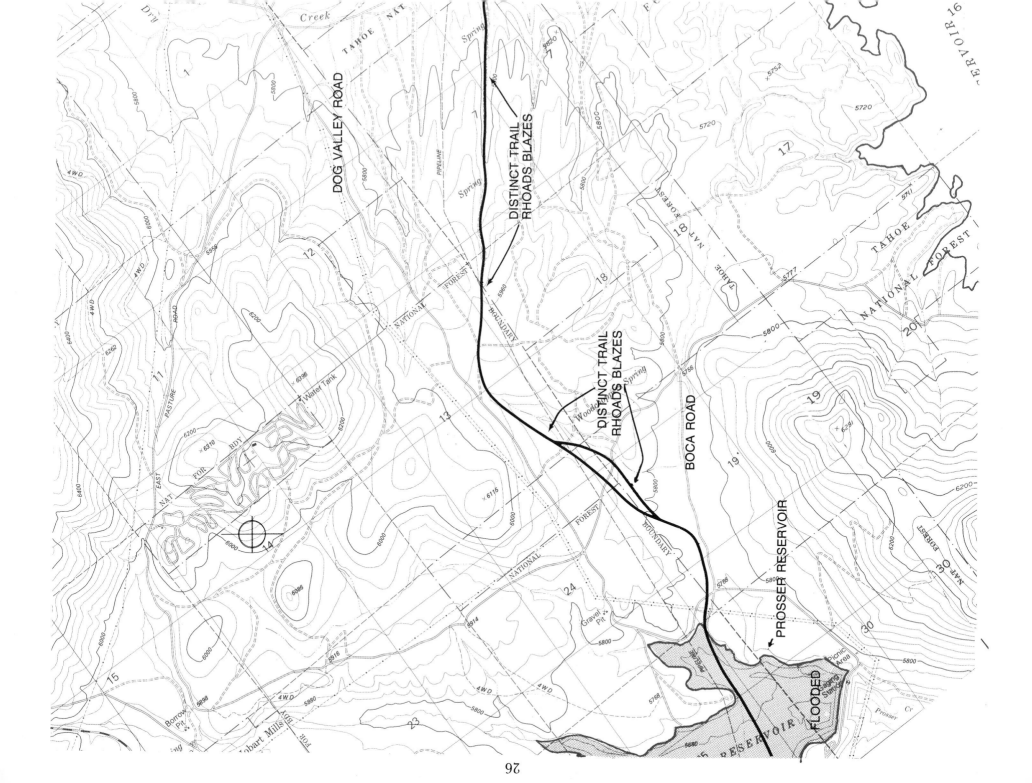

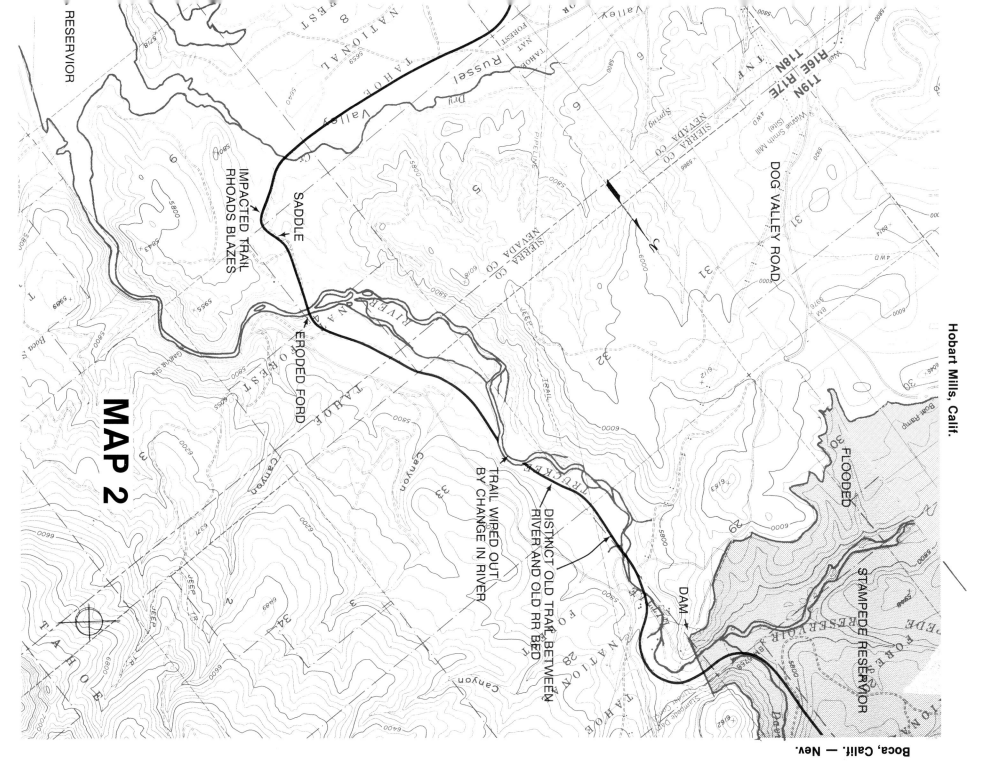

MAP 2

RESERVIOR

IMPACTED TRAIL
RHOADS BLAZES

SADDLE

ERODED FORD

TRAIL WIRED OUT
BY CHANGE IN RIVER

DISTINCT OLD TRAIL BETWEEN
RIVER AND OLD RR BED

DAM

FLOODED

STAMPEDE RESERVOIR

DOG VALLEY ROAD

Hobart Mills, Calif.

Boca, Calif. — Nev.

27

Map 2   Stampede Reservoir to Prosser Reservoir

THE RELATIVELY open terrain south of Stampede Reservoir as far as Prosser Creek would permit several wagon routes and probably several were used. The 1977 Tahoe National Forest map shows the trail closely following the old Dog Valley (Reno) Road from Dog Valley to Prosser Reservoir. Emigrant diaries mention going through this area but none gives a clear indication of where. There is an NETMC steel marker along this road just north of Russell Valley; however, because of some physical evidence found, this writer elects to describe a route confirmed by Rhoads's map.

The trail met the Little Truckee River at its confluence with Davies Creek just above the present Stampede Reservoir Dam. After crossing the Little Truckee, it turned left and followed the river through a narrow canyon now blocked by the dam. Eight hundred yards below the dam an old trail can be seen running south along the east side of the river. with an old railroad bed, abandoned in 1914, on its left. About one and one-third miles below the dam the trail and railbed have been wiped out by a shift in the river which cut deeply into its east bank for about three hundred yards. Beyond this cut a trail showing much later use continues south. Two and one-half miles below Stampede Dam it turns southwest to a ford site now badly undercut by water erosion. The trail then proceeded south-southwest up and over an eroded saddle between the Little Truckee River and the east end of Russell Valley. An impacted trail trace showing later use, marked by Rhoads's blazes, can be seen on the south side of the saddle leading down to a ford over Dry Creek in Russell Valley.

The trail swung west up the open area of Russell Valley, then turned southwest up an open draw 250 yards east of and running parallel to the pipeline shown on the map, crossing Russell Valley. A distinct old trail runs up the right side of this draw and is well-marked with Rhoads's blazes. At the top of the draw the trail is crossed by the pipeline and continues directly to a dirt road junction. It apparently joined the dirt road running southwest from this junction, then turned south down the right side of the drainage leading past Woodchopper's Spring. The eroded trail can be picked up here, where it soon crosses a gravel road just below the spring.

The clear trail continues south across a flat, open area and joins the Boca Road. From there probably continued southwest until it crossed Prosser Creek at its junction with Alder Creek. The ford used is now flooded by Prosser Reservoir, though photographs taken in 1940 clearly show this crossing.

This ford was used by emigrants at the confluence of Prosser and Alder creeks. The area is now flooded by the Prosser Reservoir.

The trail followed the east side of the Little Truckee River for 2 ½ miles.

This pine, located in the saddle between the Little Truckee River and Russell Valley, bears one of Rhoads's blazes.

Truckee, Calif.

ALDER CREEK

TAHOE-DONNER SUBDIVISION

WEDDELL SIGNS AND RHOADS BLAZES
BETWEEN PROSSER RESERVOIR AND BENNETT

Bennett Flat

FORD

Trout Creek

Gateway

Truckee

TAHOE

MAP 3

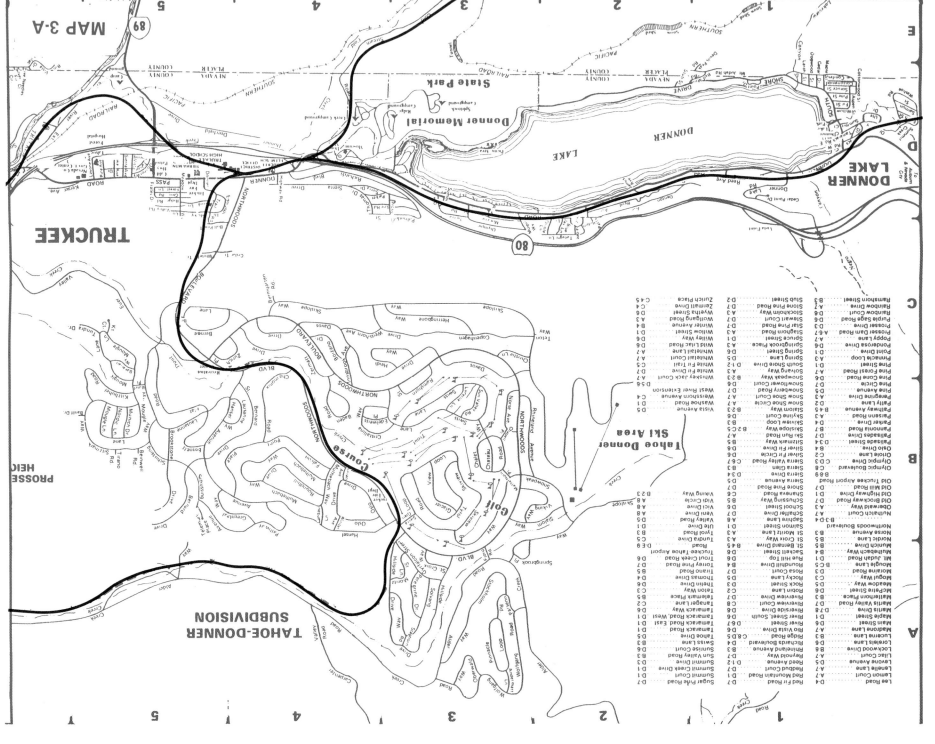

Map 3   Prosser Reservoir to Donner Lake

FOLLOWING Weddell's signs, the trail can be traced as it comes up out of the west side of Prosser Reservoir just inside the gate on the road leading north to the USFS Lakeside campground. It continues southwest up and over a low, flat-topped ridge directly to the site of George and Jacob Donner's fateful winter camp of 1846-47. This is now a U.S. Forest Service picnic area located just east of Highway 89. The large pine tree where George Donner built his lean-to is marked by a bronze plaque.

From the Donner campground the trail skirts the southeast side of a small hill and continues southwest until it crosses over the top of a deep cut on Highway 89. It then proceeds directly southwest to Alder Creek after crossing Alder Creek Drive. The trail from the Donner camp is well-defined and marked with Weddell's signs and Rhoads's blazes.

After crossing Alder Creek the trail can be traced through dense woods as it goes west along the south side of the creek. In two miles the trail bears southwest away from the creek and heads up the course of a dirt road not shown on the map. It soon leaves this road and continues south, uphill, often through heavy brush, to the Tahoe-Donner subdivision.

Map 3A on the next page shows in detail the course of the well-marked trail through the Tahoe-Donner subdivision to Tahoe-Truckee High School. A bronze plaque in front of the high school marks the trail.

From the vicinity of the high school the trail went to the east end of Donner Lake. Here it passes present Donner Memorial Park and Museum, which mark the site of the main camp of the Donner party in the winter of 1846-47. The diaries of emigrants who passed through after this tragedy contain comments on the utter desolation and horror of the Donner campsites both here and at Alder Creek.

The route from the crossing of Prosser Creek to Donner Lake as described above is accepted by most historians as the emigrant trail. Historical evidence, however, indicates that a more direct and much easier route was used as early as 1845. After crossing Prosser Creek it went generally along the Dog Valley Road (later old Highway 89) to the Truckee River at present Truckee and thence to Donner Lake. In 1849 John Markle wrote in his diary: "The first two miles brought us to the valley where Donner encamped. One mile more brought us opposite to where the cabins were, which were situated one or two miles from the road on the right-hand side. Six miles more and we came to where the Graves family (Donner Party) wintered." From a point where the old Dog Valley road comes up out of the Prosser Reservoir near a boat ramp (S½ Sec. 25, T18N, R16E) the Donner campsite can be seen one and one-half miles to the right. From this point it is six miles by the most direct route to the Graves cabin site, which is adjacent to the Truckee agricultural inspection station on I-80.

In 1845 Jacob Snyder wrote: "We struck Truckeys River and encamped about one mile from the point where we struck it. Near the point where we struck it are two large isolated rocks in the valley." Snyder's diary goes on to indicate that the next day they followed the river on the right side until they "struck" a lake well-described as Donner Lake. There is one large rock in Truckee behind the Truckee Hotel just east of the street junction where Highway 267 turns south to cross the Southern Pacific tracks. Another large rock is just south of it along the railroad tracks. There is little doubt that these unique rock formations are the ones referred to by Jacob Snyder.

A study of the terrain plus the evidence cited above and elsewhere provides convincing evidence that at least one branch of the trail avoided the Alder-Trout Creek dogleg and went through present Truckee to reach Donner Lake as shown on Map 3. It may have been used exclusively once it was once established.

This blaze was placed by Rhoads near Alder Creek.

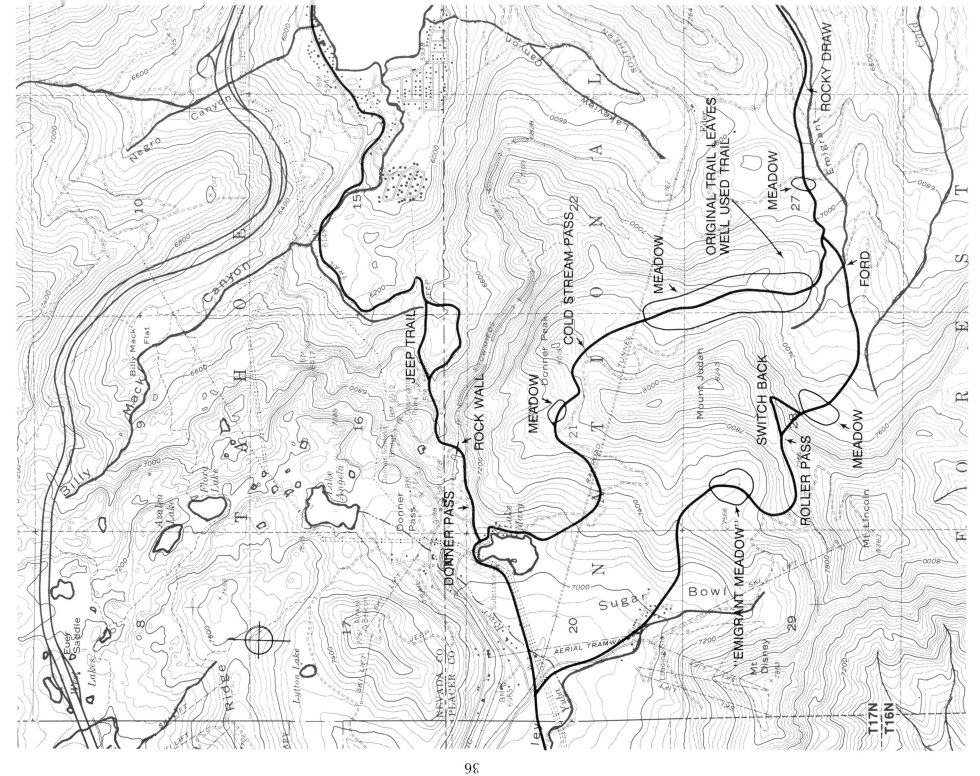

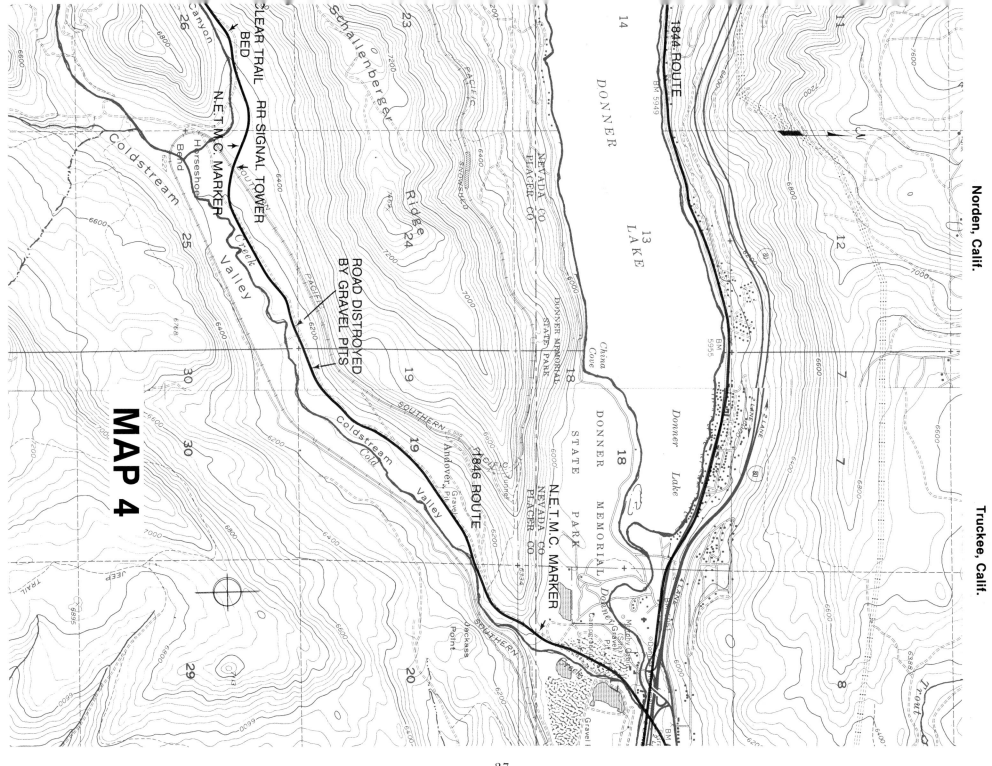

MAP 4

CLEAR TRAIL RR SIGNAL TOWER BED

N.E.T.M.C. MARKER

Horseshoe Bend

Coldstream Canyon

Schallenberger Ridge

PACIFIC

NEVADA CO PLACER CO

SNOWSHED

ROAD DISTROYED BY GRAVEL PITS

Coldstream Creek Valley

PACIFIC

23

24

25

26

14

DONNER LAKE 13

BM 5949

1844 ROUTE

11

12

DONNER MEMORIAL STATE PARK

China Cove

Donner Lake

BM 5955

N

30

30

29

19

19

18

18

7

7

8

SOUTHERN

Andover Pit

Gravel

Coldstream Cold Valley

1846 ROUTE

PACIFIC

NEVADA CO PLACER CO

Tunnel

DONNER STATE PARK MEMORIAL

N.E.T.M.C. MARKER

Mosby

Gravel Pit

Donner Creek

Campground

2 LANE

BM

6388

Trout

Jackass Point

SOUTHERN

20

+5334

Gravel Pit

80

80

2 LANE

2 LANE

JEEP TRAIL

6895

713

Map 4   The Three Summit Passes

The Trail from Donner Lake via Donner Pass to Summit Valley

IN 1846 EDWIN BRYANT wrote in his diary: "To mount this [Donner Pass] was our next difficulty. Standing at the bottom and looking upwards at the perpendicular, and in some places impending, granite cliffs, the observer, without any further knowledge on the subject, would doubt that man or beast ever made good a passage over them."

The east side of the pass has been badly defaced by blasting and grading for the Central Pacific Railroad and a succession of roads, including the Dutch Flat-Donner Lake Wagon Road, the Victory Highway, and Highway 40. The Pacific Telephone underground cable and gas pipeline were also blasted through this area. Consequently, there is little remaining physical evidence that can be positively identified as the original crossing. Furthermore, only a few emigrants used this pass.

It is generally believed, and it would seem logical from detailed ground reconnaissance, that the Dutch Flat-Donner Lake Wagon Road initially followed the old trail toward the pass. This road went along the north side of Donner Lake and from there initially took the general course of the jeep trail on the map, along the south side of the stream flowing down the pass. Whether the emigrant trail continued up the jeep trail or took some other course has yet to be determined.

A location was found which fits a description in Schallenberger's story: "The worst place was about halfway up where there was a vertical rock about ten feet high. They managed to find a little rift in the rock and through it they forced the oxen one by one. Then they yoked the oxen again, put chains down to the wagons . . . brought the wagons one by one over the ledge." In the SW¼ of

SE¼ of Section 16, just north of the streambed, signs of an old trail defaced by pipeline grading end abruptly at the base of an almost vertical, smooth-faced, worn rock about twelve to fifteen feet high. A narrow rift is at the left of this rock. Above the rock a well-defined but presently unused trail continues up the path.

The only ungraded wagon access to the top of the pass was through a V-shaped gap now blocked by fill and faced with a rock wall laid by Chinese workers to support the Central Pacific Railroad tracks. The final approach to this gap was across a granite incline sloping up immediately to the right of the streambed.

Beyond the tracks the trail followed the trace of an unimproved road running west over the top of the pass, where it soon joined the improved road (see map) leading to Lake Mary. Just east of the highest point is a bronze marker stating "Stephens [Stevens] Pass Emigrant Trail," put up by the E Clampus Vitus organization in 1979. Rust-stained, worn rocks were found on a dirt road which closely followed the north end of Lake Mary. Edwin Bryant refers to Lake Mary in this way: "A mile [from the summit] brought us to a small dimple on the top of the mountain in the center of which is a miniature lake, surrounded by green grass."

The trail probably went west from the lake down the course of the present power line until it was joined by the trail over the Lincoln-Judah pass, At this point the power line crosses the road into the Sugar Bowl ski area. From there the trail went west down the draw into Summit Valley.

ROLLER PASS

COLD STREAM PASS

DONNER PASS

This photo defines the three summit passes of the Truckee Route.

This plaque at the top of Donner Pass honors the Stevens-Townsend-Murphy party. There was an attempt some years ago to have the name changed to Stevens Pass.

The trail up Donner Pass went through a gap which now is blocked by a rock retaining wall. The barrier was erected in 1866 to support the tracks of the Central Pacific Railroad.

The Donner monument in Donner Memorial State Park is near the point where Moses Schallenberger and his companions built their cabin in the winter of 1844-45. The cabin was occupied by the Breen family of the Donner Party two years later. The height of the base of the monument is the same as the snow level that awful winter.

The Trail from Donner Lake up Cold Stream Valley and Emigrant Canyon

THE SAME TRAIL WAS USED to approach both Roller and Cold Stream passes up to a point in Emigrant Canyon about one mile east of the summit.

This common trail went south from the vicinity of Donner Memorial Park and crossed the Donner Lake outlet stream to the entrance to Cold Stream Valley. An NETMC steel marker is on a knob at the valley entrance between the unimproved road, noted on the map, and a new paved haul road. Evidence of the old trail can be seen extending about 300 yards beyond this point between the two roads until the road on the left converges with it. Shortly beyond, the original face of the valley floor has been completely defaced by gravel operations that extend over a mile up the valley. Beyond the gravel pits the original unimproved road, as shown on the map, can be picked up. Weddell's signs, previously erected but now gone, marked this road as the trace of the emigrant trail to within one-half mile of the apex of the Horse Shoe Bend of the Southern Pacific Railroad. There the faint trail, clearly marked by Weddell's signs, leaves the road and angles right up to the Southern Pacific tracks at Signal Tower #2022. An NETMC steel marker is 120 yards up the slope west of the signal tower. Weddell's trail signs indicate that about one-fifth mile farther west the old trail was joined by a dirt road not shown on the map. This road soon joins the unimproved road, shown on the map running west along the north side of Emigrant Canyon Creek. The well-defined trail can be seen along the south side of this road for about one-fifth mile until the two converge. One-third mile farther on, the trail again leaves the road to follow closely the north side of the creek. After another one-third mile, it turns northwest up a steep, wooded, rocky draw until it crosses the road up the canyon about one-tenth mile west of its junction with the road to Eder. After crossing a

Weather and time are wearing away at the few remaining P. M. Weddell trail signs. All are badly deteriorated and will soon be gone.

bulldozed area the deeply eroded trail can be found leading west up a moderate slope. About one-fourth mile beyond the road crossing, the eroded trail traverses a granite outcropping where it soon intercepts a wide logging road. This road swings to the left of a small meadow, at the center of Section 27, T17N, R15E. Two of Weddell's signs indicate that the trail left the road there and crossed the meadow going west.

The well-defined trail is picked up west of the meadow beyond a cleared-out area, where it takes a zig zag course up increasingly steeper terrain, generally parallel to Emigrant Canyon Creek. This section is well-marked by Weddell's signs and shows considerable use by hikers. About one-third mile west of the meadow the trail turns sharply south over a granite outcropping. Approximately 150 yards south of this turn there is a long-unused natural ford at the center of the SW ¼ of Section 27. This ford appears to be one used on the trail to the Lincoln-Judah pass, while the trail to the Judah-Donner Peak pass continues up the north side of Emigrant Canyon.

The trail to Cold Stream Pass crossed this beautiful mountain meadow on the east side of Mount Judah heading northwest. Here Amos took time to smell the flowers.

The Trail from Emigrant Canyon Over the Mount Judah-Donner Peak Pass (Cold Stream Pass) to Summit Valley

THE TRAIL TO THE PASS between Mount Judah and Donner Peak branches off from the trail to the Lincoln-Judah Pass in the vicinity of the ford mentioned above. The well-used trail continues up the north side of Emigrant Canyon Creek. One-quarter mile above the ford, Weddell's signs indicate that the original trail turned northwest off the presently traveled trail up a steep draw to a series of broad meadows. From these meadows, which skirt the east side of Mount Judah, Donner Lake can be seen. After passing three-quarters of a mile north through the meadows, the trail enters a wooded draw with a stream on its right. From here it is overgrown, rocky, and hard to find. The direction of the draw suggests and several rust-stained rocks confirm the northwest course of the trail. It soon swings west up the pass between Mount Judah and Donner Peak, where the final climb is from twenty to twenty-five degrees. The pass is marked by the remains of a rock cairn put up by Weddell in 1924, by a Nevada Emigrant Trail Marking Committee steel marker, and by a large white sign (origin unknown) which reads "Emigrant Trail Truckee River Route, Cold Stream, Elevation 7,812 ft."

From the pass the trail can be seen going west down a draw north of and parallel to the unimproved road shown on the map. One-quarter mile below the pass it joins the road briefly, then veers off to the right again and soon crosses a small meadow. Weddell's signs follow the trail from here around the northwest shoulder of Mount Judah, initially along the road for about 200 yards. It then drops steeply off the road near a huge stump on the uphill side.

From here no evidence of the trail remains because of heavy logging. A few deteriorated Weddell signs and Rhoads blazes set the course on a steep downhill traverse in a southwesterly direction, first crossing the Pacific Crest Trail and next, one-third mile below, a switchback in the road. It then proceeds down an eroded rocky draw in a northwest direction to the foot of the mountain. This draw is well-marked with Weddell's signs, a tree showing snub marks and worn, rust-marked rocks.

The trail comes to the flat 150 yards south of Lake Mary and the last Weddell trail sign appears near the southernmost house in the small community on the east side of the lake. From here the trail apparently went around the north side of the lake, where it joins the earlier one coming over Donner Pass.

The Trail from Emigrant Canyon Over the Mount Lincoln-Mount Judah Pass (Roller Pass) to Summit Valley

Halfway up the last slope of Roller Pass

ROLLER PASS IS BY FAR the most spectacular of the several passes over the Sierra and is well worth visiting. In 1846 Elisha Perkins described its appearance this way: ''As we came up to it the appearances was exactly like marching up to some immense wall built directly across our path, so perpendicular is this dividing ridge. . . .''

The trail to Roller Pass branched off from the Coldstream Pass trail near the ford mentioned earlier. Across the ford in the direction of Roller Pass is an intensely logged area where there is little chance of finding clear evidence of the old trail. It is apparent that the wide, relatively easy slope lends itself to any number of routes until shortly before it reaches a meadow at the foot of the pass. Here the California Beaches and Parks Survey of 1950 indicates that the trail made a sweep to the south, then turned northwest as it reached the meadow. This route avoids the steep approach to the meadow from due east.

After using the meadow as a staging area, the emigrants originally pulled their wagons one by one up a thirty-degree slope for approximately 400 feet to the top of the 7,860-foot pass by using a log roller on the lip of the pass. It acted as a bearing for chains connecting multiple yokes of oxen at the crest with a wagon below. Some wagon parties used additional chains running up to and around the roller to permit other oxen to pull downhill.

Mary A. Jones in 1846 vividly described her party's ascent of the pass as follows: ''Bye and Bye we reached the great mountain and pitched our tent at the foot of it. In the morning my husband got up and looked out and said, 'Mary, it is snowing and we are doomed

At times, hundreds of wagons were forced to wait in this small meadow just below Roller Pass. They turned at this point to cross the pass during the gold rush.

to stay in this place all winter.' I said, 'Oh, no. It will quit snowing pretty soon,' and we got up the mountain before dark. I carried one baby and led the other most all the way up. The way we climbed the mountain, we hitched nine or ten yokes of oxen to a wagon and drove them as far as they could go, and a chain that worked over a roller on the top of the mountain and a man on each wheel did the work.''

At the northwest end of the meadow an open corridor through the trees leads up to the pass. The top of the pass is marked by a U.S. Forest Service sign.

Elisha Perkins describes a later switchback trail to the summit as follows: ''The road going up to the base turns short to the right and ascends by a track cut in the side of the mountains till two-thirds up when it turns left again and goes directly to the summit.'' This cut was made by a large party that took time to grade diagonally up the slope to the right of the original ascent. It traversed an open twenty-five-degree slope of loose rock for about 150 yards in a north-northeast direction until it reached a wooded shelf. Continuing in the same direction for another 250 yards, it turned directly uphill just short of a dry wash, which is 400 yards northeast of the lip of the original pass. It then made a ninety-degree left turn and headed back to the original pass across a level granite shoulder just below a line of trees. No evidence of the lower leg of the traverse can be found until it reaches the wooded shelf. Many rust-scarred rocks can be seen there and on the upper traverse. This traverse joins the top of the original pass fifty yards east of the present Pacific Crest Trail.

Just west of the top of the pass the trail takes a sharp turn to the southwest on a shallow downhill traverse. Within 200 yards it is lost in a grove of stunted pines, but 150 yards later it breaks out into an open rocky shelf strewn with telltale rust-stained rocks just below the ridge line. The trail soon drops downhill to the northwest and is lost in the open Sugar Bowl ski area on the northwest shoulder of Mount Lincoln. It then swings north-northwest through ''Emigrant Meadow.'' Reference is made in Mary A. Jones's diary to a watering place in this meadowabout a mile west of the pass. From there the trail apparently went northwest, passing near Sugar Bowl Lodge at the foot of the mountain and then converged on the trail from Donner Pass east of Summit Valley.

47

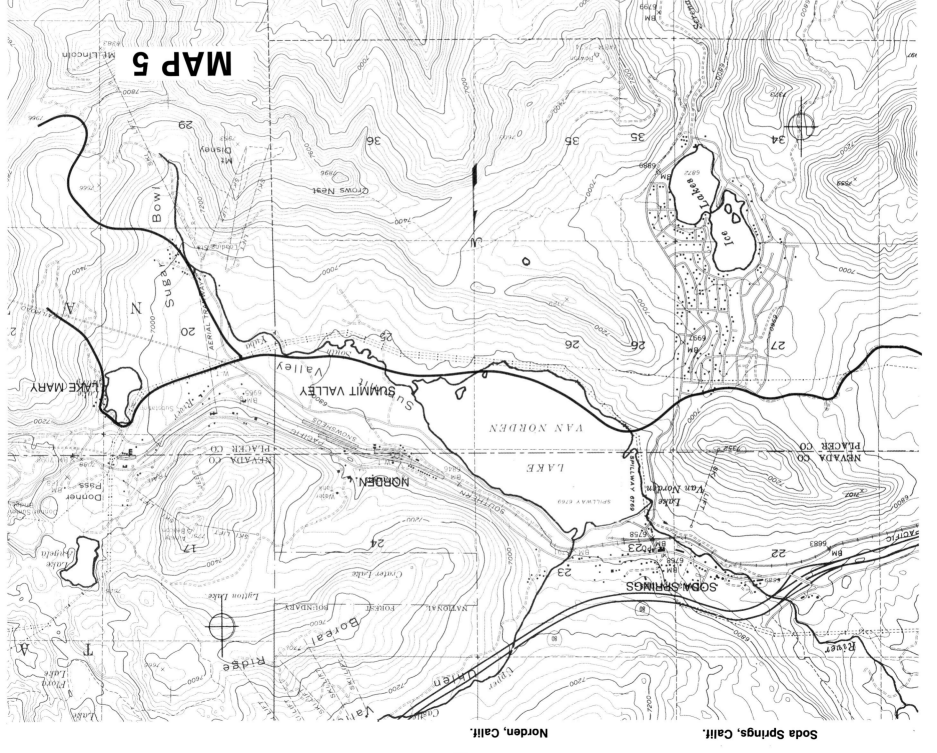

MAP 5

Map 5   Summit Valley

SUMMIT VALLEY IS NOW partially flooded by Lake Van Norden, which is near Soda Springs. This beautiful valley is identified in many diaries as a welcome resting place after the tortuous summit crossing.

In 1849 Wakeman Bryarly best expressed the feelings of the emigrants on their arrival there: ''We passed through a grove of woods and then emerged into a beautiful valley and encamped. We were all in the most joyous & elated spirits this evening. We have crossed the only part of road that we feared, & that without any breakage, loss or detention. I had but the one & only bottle of 'cognac' that was in our camp, & which I had managed to keep since leaving the Old Dominion. This I invited my mess to join me in, & which invitation was most cordially accepted. When lo & behold, upon bringing it out, it was empty — yes positively empty. The cork was bad & with numerous joltings, it had gradually disappeared. This was a disappointment many of us will not soon forget.''

Summit Valley — where the emigrants rested after crossing the crest

This flat, boulder-strewn area was described by Micajah Littleton.

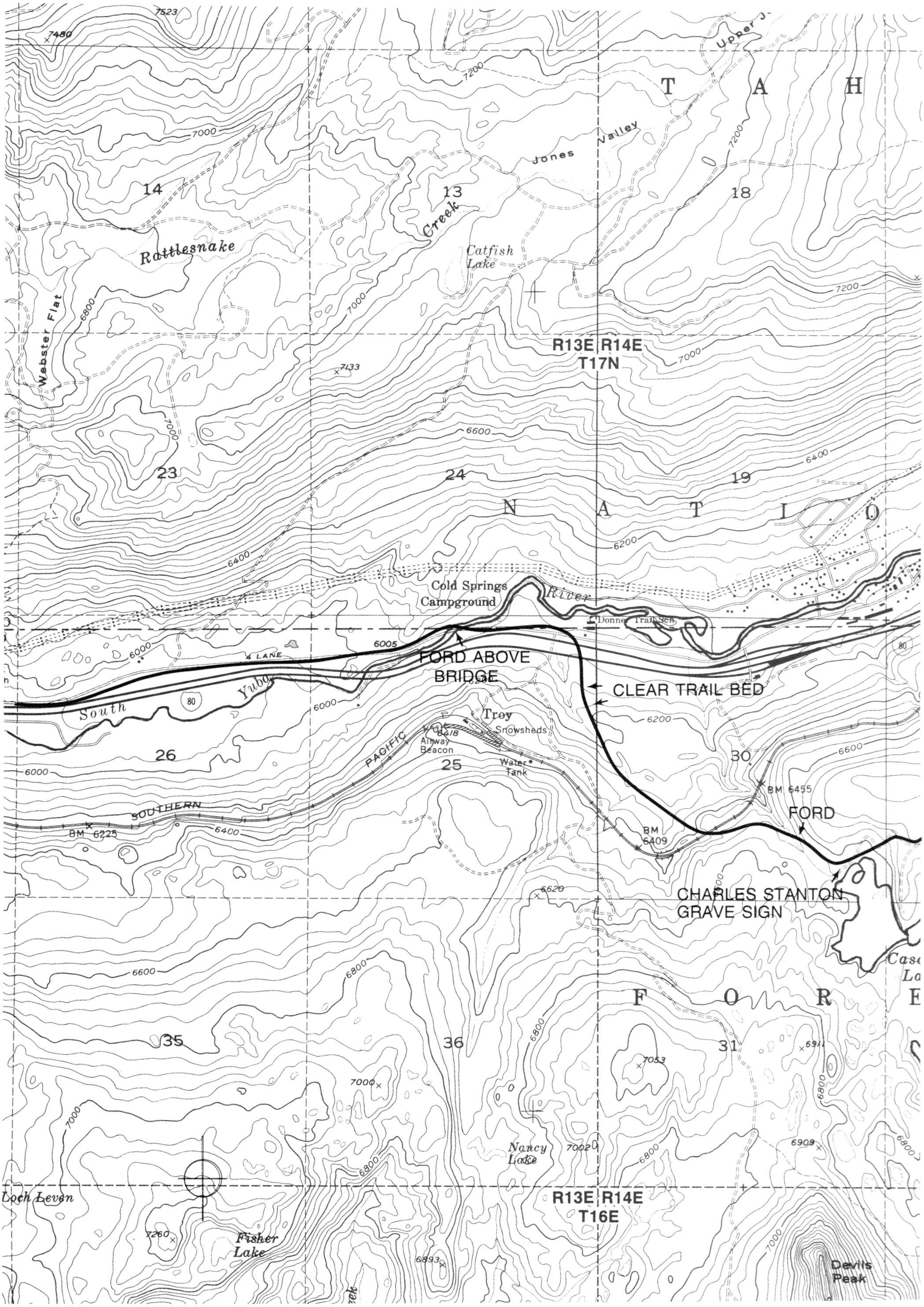

T A H O E

N A T I O N A L

F O R E S T

Devils Peak

Upper

Jones Valley

Catfish Lake

Creek

Rattlesnake

Webster Flat

18

19

30

31

13

24

25

36

14

23

26

35

R13E R14E
T17N

R13E R14E
T16E

FORD

CHARLES STANTON
GRAVE SIGN

CLEAR TRAIL BED

FORD ABOVE
BRIDGE

Cold Springs
Campground

Donner Trail

Troy

Snowsheds

Water
Tank

Airway
Beacon

PACIFIC

SOUTHERN

South Yuba River

4 LANE

Nancy Lake

Fisher Lake

Loch Leven

BM 6455

BM 6409

BM 6225

80

80

6800

6909

7053

7133

7523

7450

MAP 6

COUNTY ROAD

DRY-STREAM BED

NEVADA CO
PLACER CO

SOUTHERN PACIFIC

(NORDEN)
1962 IV SE

NORDEN 1.2 MI.
RENO, NEV. 45 MI.

SPILLWAY 6769

Map 6 Summit Valley to the South Yuba River

FROM THE SOUTHWEST END of Summit Valley the trail turned south up a ravine on the left side of the present road running south out of Soda Springs. Near the top of a low gap by Cascade Road, the trail turned west, then generally followed Pahatsi Road into the Royal Gorge Nordic Ski Resort Lodge trail entrance. From here the trail went west along the course of the county road, as shown on the map. There are several lakes throughout the area. In 1850 M. Littleton, in desribing this unique area wrote: "The rock is all through the wood looking like waggons, white cows and sheep."

After passing between Kilborn and Kidd lakes, the trail continued around the north side of Kidd Lake. There is some doubt among researchers as to the route(s) taken from here down to the South Yuba River. Bert Wiley has indicated that the trail turns northwest just west of the Kidd Lake drainage and drops down to the Southern Pacific Railroad tracks and I-80, where it bottoms out just west of the California Transportation Division buildings at Kingvale.

Another more frequently described route traces the trail south along the west side of Kidd Lake to the end of the county road just above Cascade Lakes. From there it turns right and follows the course of a dirt road down a rock outcrop to a small flat below the dam at the northwest end of Cascade Lakes. On the flat is a U.S. Forest Service sign marking the approximate location of the grave of Charles Stanton of the Donner Party. About 150 yards beyond this sign an old trail can be found swinging northwest off a dirt road and following down the right side of the Cascade Lakes drainage

One of Wendell Robie's "Mountain Lions" metal trail signs can be seen above a blaze and wagon hub marks at the rear of the Big Bend Ranger Station. Only ten of the 100-odd signs he placed in 1934 have been found by the author. Most of these have been vandalized.

stream. For one-fourth mile several worn and rust-stained rocks can be seen as well as the characteristic impacted trailbed until it reaches a ford. On the west side of the ford the trail is lost in a logged-out area that extends below the Southern Pacific Railroad tracks to I-80. However, following the general direction of an unnamed trail in the Government Land Office 1866 survey in a northwest direction, a section of trail beginning one-third mile south of I-80, directly south of Donner Trail School, shows characteristic impaction, rust stains on rocks, and rocks moved to the side.

No original trail evidence was found along the South Yuba River between Kingvale and Hampshire Rocks. The valley floor has been drastically altered by road construction since emigrant days. It is known from diaries that it was one of the worst sections of trail the emigrants had to negotiate. John Markle described it as "indescribable and the damndest, rockiest and roughest road I ever saw."

Diaries mentioned a crossing of the South Yuba after the descent into the valley. The river along here is characterized by rough, rocky banks and a boulder-strewn streambed. The most likely ford site is just above the old Highway 40 bridge one-half mile below the Donner Trail School. All signs of a ford on the east bank have been obliterated by grading for the road approach to the bridge. However, on the west bank a narrow, sandy, easy grade comes directly up into the old Cold Springs campground about 100 yards above the bridge. There is another possible fording site 300 yards below the old Highway 40 bridge.

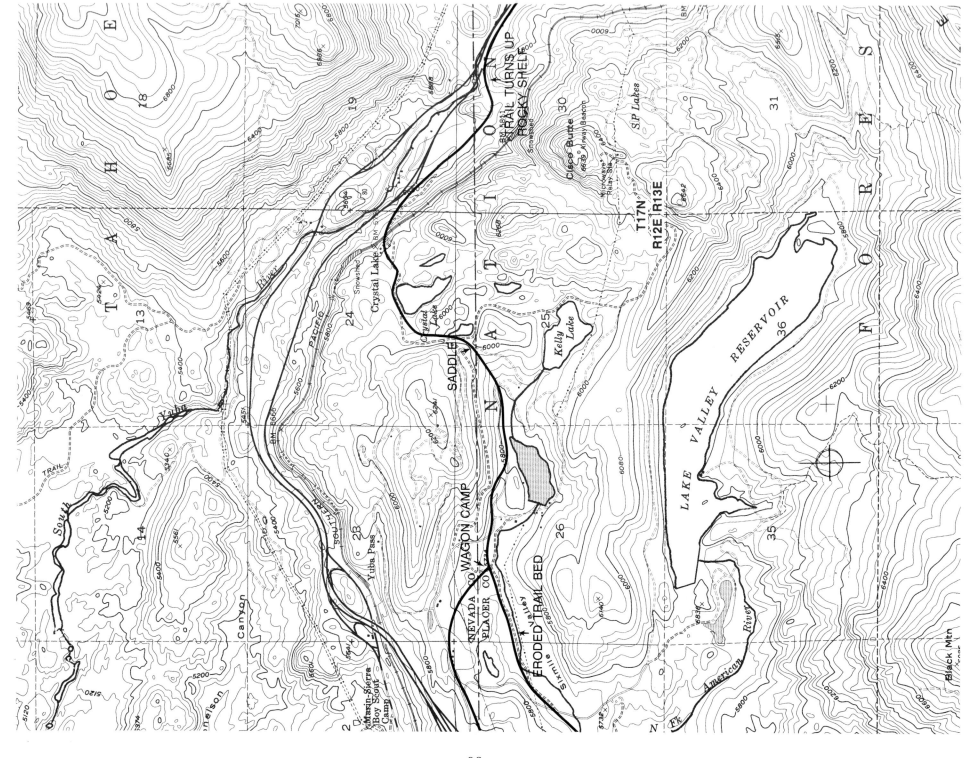

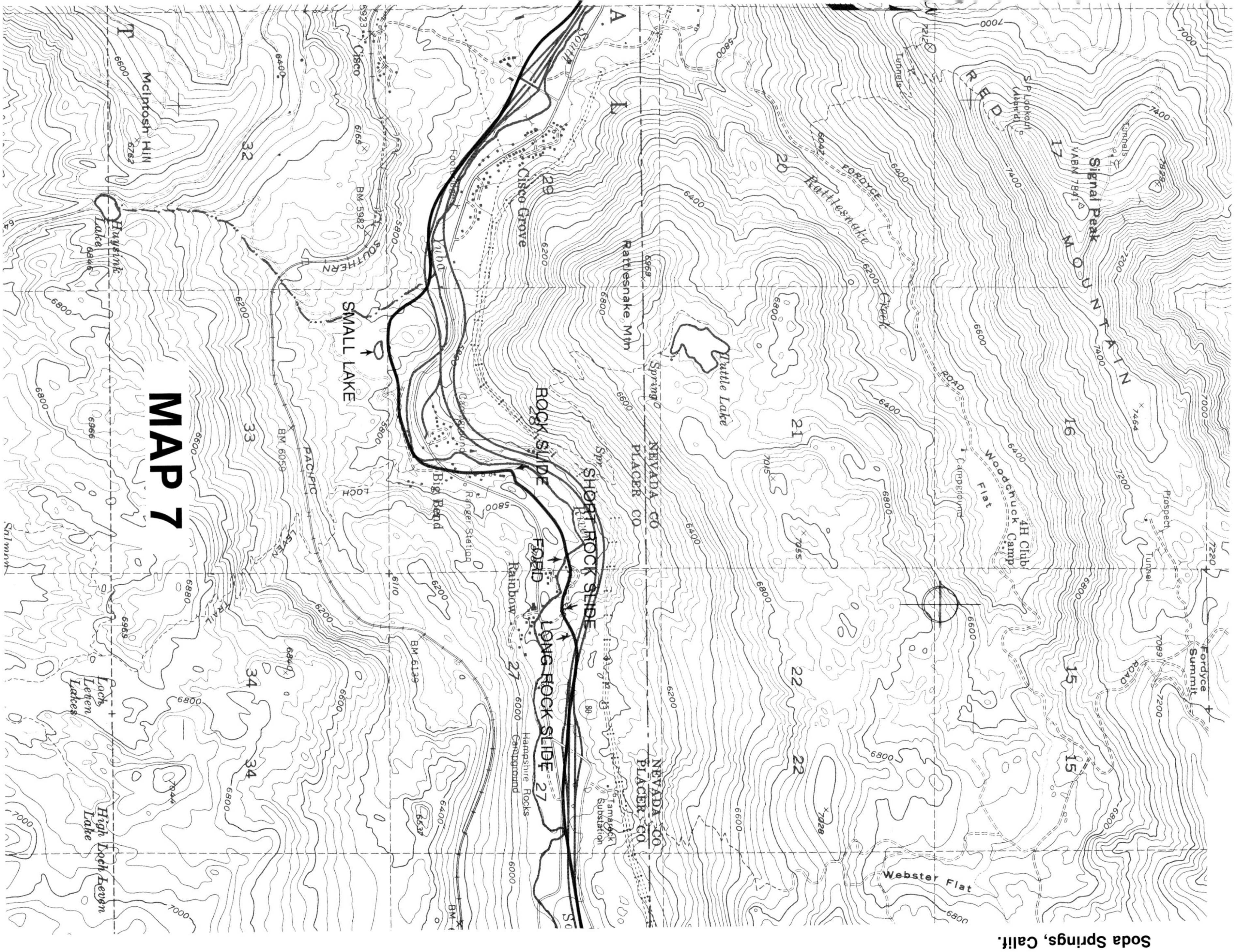
MAP 7
Cisco Grove, Calif.
Soda Springs, Calif.
SMALL LAKE
ROCK SLIDE
SHORT ROCK SLIDE
LONG ROCK SLIDE
FORD
Cisco Grove
Cisco
Rattlesnake Mtn
Rattlesnake Creek
Tuttle Lake
Signal Peak
RED MOUNTAIN
Woodchuck Flat
4H Club Camp
Campground
Big Bend
Ranger Station
Rainbow
Hampshire Rocks
Campground
Tamarack Substation
Webster Flat
McIntosh Hill
Huysink Lake
Loch Leven Lakes
High Loch Leven Lake
Fordyce Summit
NEVADA CO
PLACER CO
SOUTHERN
PACIFIC
LOCH LEVEN TRAIL
FORDYCE ROAD

Map 7   Hampshire Rocks to Six Mile Valley

AFTER FOLLOWING DOWN THE NORTH SIDE of the South Yuba River, the wagon trains crossed to the south side to avoid the steep slope north of Big Bend. After first crossing a wide granite outcropping at Hampshire Rocks northeast of Rainbow Lodge, they used a steep rocky slide to get to a small flat above the river. This slide begins 200 yards west of the present Rainbow turnoff from the eastbound lane of I-80. It can be identified by a tall stone chimney located partway down the chute which is choked with boulders and fallen timber. To the west, across the small flat at the bottom, a much shorter slide was used to reach the riverbank. In addition to worn granite, this slide can be identified by a ''Mt. Lions'' trail sign on a brush-hidden stump near the top and another on a pine tree at the bottom.

The trail then followed the north bank of the river directly across from Rainbow Lodge for a short distance before crossing over. The well-defined crossing point at the end of an unimproved road is noted on the map. The trail can be found about 300 yards west of the crossing as it traverses over the flat rock surfaces on the north side of a high granite knob 350 yards northeast of the Big Bend Ranger Station. ''Mt. Lions'' trail signs, hub-scarred trees and rust-stained rocks mark the trail.

About 260 yards northeast of the Big Bend Ranger Station the trail turned abruptly to the right down a short granite slope toward the river bottom. Rust-stained and worn rocks clearly mark this slope. From here the trail turned left past the ranger station where a California State Historical Trail plaque marks the trace of the trail. Across old Highway 40 the trail followed the south bank of the river around a bend on a course that later became the Dutch Flat-Donner Lake Wagon Road, which can still be seen going through the Big Bend settlement.

This California State Overland Emigrant Trail plaque is in front of the Big Bend Ranger Station.

The trail soon avoids another narrow river canyon by crossing a saddle between Big Bend and Cisco. To the right of a USFS "Big Granite Trail" sign are indications of an old trail leading to a draw near the top of the saddle. At the top of the draw are the clearest marker rocks yet found on the trail. An overgrown old trail follows close along the north side of a small lake. Once over the saddle, a very distinct trail showing considerably more recent use leads northwest, down along the east side of the Huysink Lake drainage until it becomes obliterated by I-80. A "Mt. Lions" trail sign is just south of the highway.

The trail then apparently followed the south bank of the South Yuba to a point .7 miles northwest of the Cisco Road crossing of I-80, where it again left the river to avoid a steep canyon. Just short of the Placer-Nevada County line the old Dutch Flat-Donner Lake Wagon Road grade can be clearly seen heading southwest around a granite shoulder away from I-80. Immediately above, the original trail parallels it up a steep rocky shelf and crosses over a shoulder. Although eroded and overgrown with bushes in places, worn rocks are still in evidence. More marker rocks indicate that the trail went down a draw directly toward Cisco Butte, then turned northwest where it soon tied in with the Old Dutch Flat-Donner Lake Wagon Road again. This road goes northwest along a draw at the foot of Cisco Butte until it breaks out into Indian Springs Flat immediately southeast of the eastbound Eagle Lakes turnoff of I-80.

The California State Beaches and Parks report shows the trail generally following the unimproved road on the map, which is also the route of the Dutch Flat-Donner Lake Wagon Road, from Indian Springs up past the west side of Crystal Lake. Below and parallel to this road going up out of the flat is an old roadbed following a natural shelf, which appears to be an ungraded approach up the side of the mountain. It was used to route the Pacific Telephone cable, which obliterates any chance of positive identification of the old trail.

About 100 yards above the first sharp left turn of the road above the Southern Pacific Railroad tracks, an old trail can be seen leading to the right through some old ruins. Beyond them a draw strewn with junk leads to several rust-stained, worn rocks. Farther on, the draw is overgrown but soon leads to a well-defined trail which rejoins the road below Crystal Lake. A California State Historical Trail marker locates the course of the trail along the west side of Crystal Lake.

After passing the lake, the trail went south up through a saddle where there is now the privately owned "Snowflower Development" campground. From there it dropped down the center of a draw into Six Mile Valley where, until recently, artifacts of a large emigrant camping area, including wagon parts and discarded camp articles, could be found. Evidence of the trail is found below the saddle, along the right side of the road leading down past the Snowflower Lodge and later, across the open part of the lower valley.

Overland Emigrant Trail marker at Crystal Lake

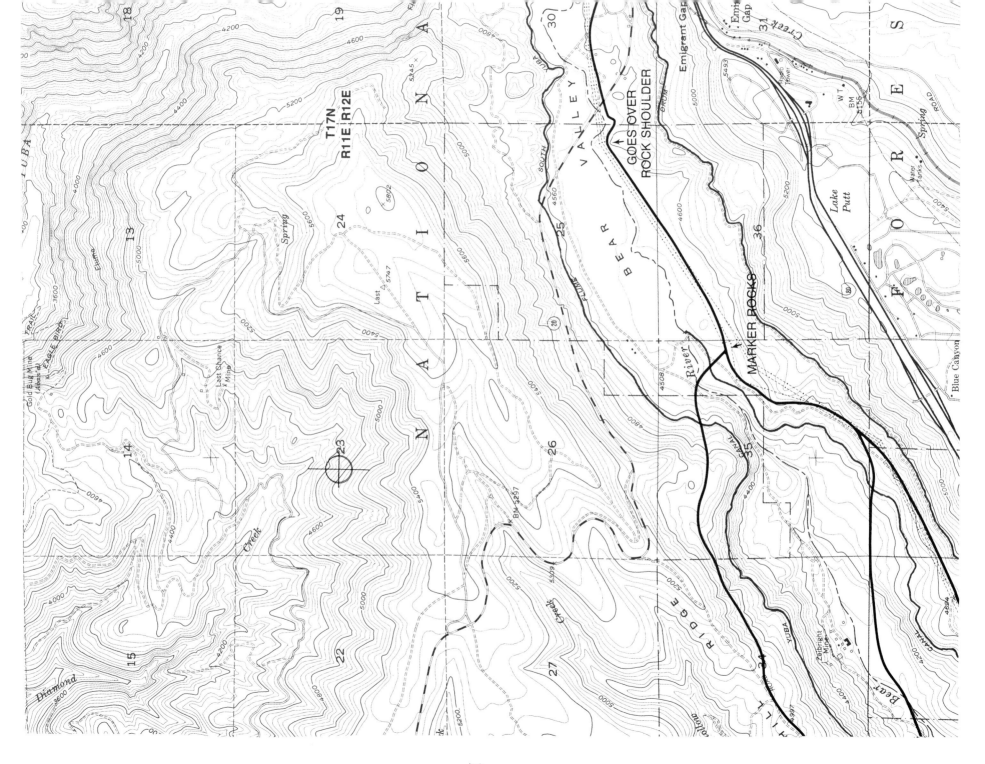

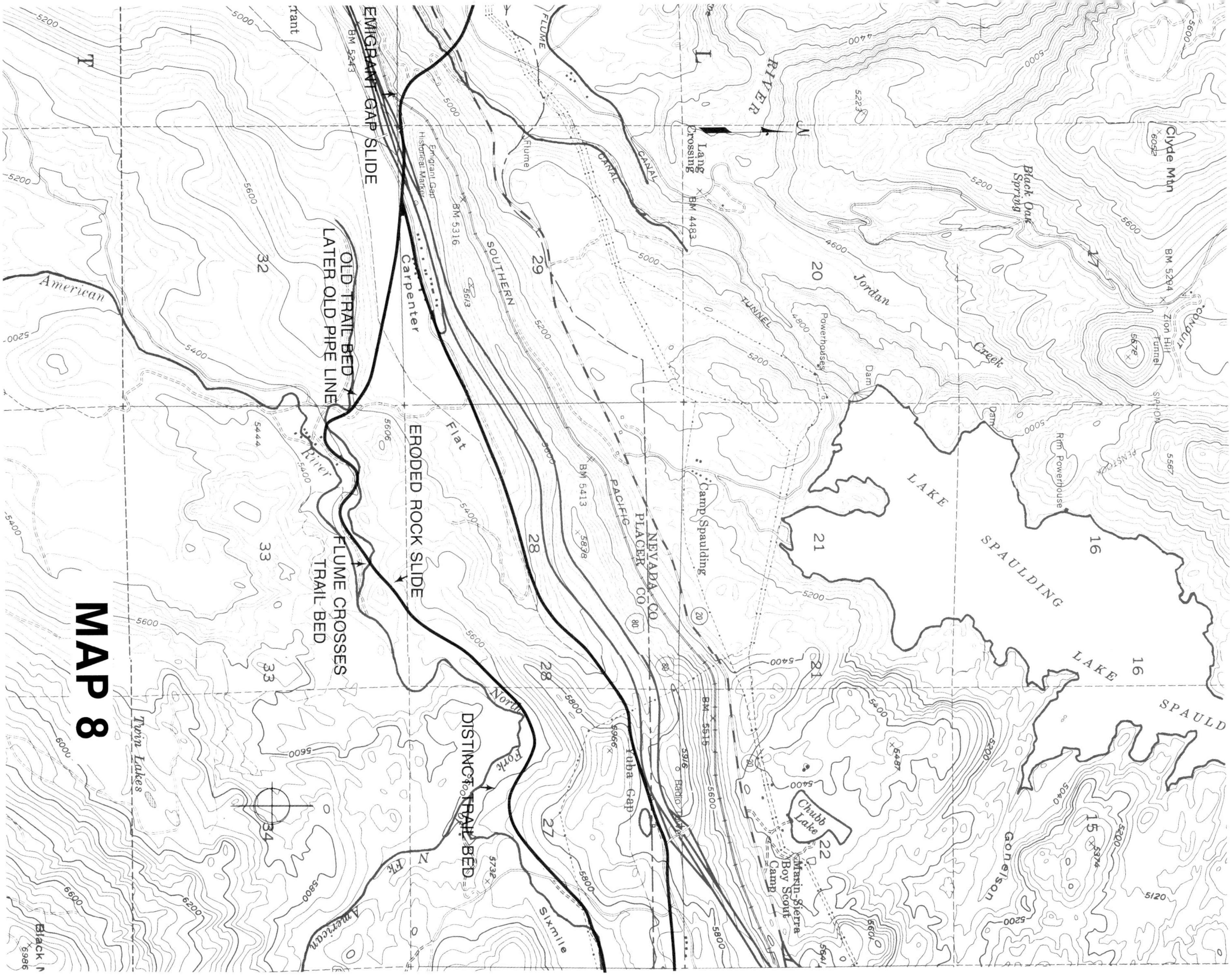

MAP 8

EMIGRANT GAP SLIDE

OLD TRAIL BED
LATER OLD PIPE LINE

ERODED ROCK SLIDE

FLUME CROSSES
TRAIL BED

DISTINCT TRAIL BED

Emigrant Gap
Historical Marker

Carpenter

Flat

River

American

Twin Lakes

North Fork

American

N Fk

Sixmile

Black

SOUTHERN

PACIFIC

NEVADA CO.

PLACER CO.

Yuba Gap

Radio

FLUME

CANAL

CANAL

TUNNEL

CONDUIT

TUNNEL

Lang
Crossing

RIVER

Jordan

Creek

Powerhouse

Dam

Camp Spaulding

LAKE

SPAULDING

LAKE

SPAULD

SPAULD

Clyde Mtn

Black Oak
Spring

Zion Hill

Rm Powerhouse

PENSTOCK

Goethson

Chubb
Lake

Marin Sierra
Boy Scout
Camp

BM 5243

BM 5316

5663

5606

5444

5413

3878

3946

BM 5515

BM 4483

6052

5223

BM 5294

5676

5567

5966

3732

5887

5374

5120

6986

32

33

33

34

29

28

28

28

27

20

21

21

22

17

16

16

15

63

Map 8   Six Mile Valley to Bear Valley

BEGINNING ABOUT 100 YARDS west of the Yuba Gap-Lake Valley Reservoir Road and just north of the Six Mile Valley drainage, clear indications of the impacted trail are found generally following the north side of, first, the drainage creek and then the north fork of the North Fork of the American River. The trail alternately crosses low wooded areas and granite outcroppings along here and shows considerable later use.

About one and one-third miles beyond the Lake Valley Reservoir Road, the trail turns down to the river, where it now looks like a badly eroded draw leading down the west side of a granite knob. At the bottom it is crossed by a flume 100 yards below a small dam. Below the flume an old trail can be seen running southwest for about 200 yards until it joins the unimproved road running generally west to a saddle at the road junction on the boundary of Sections 32 and 33, T17N R12E. About 150 yards below the saddle a trail covered with debris and brush turns off the road to the left down a draw running northwest into Carpenter Flat. This draw was used later for a now-abandoned water pipeline.

There is some indication from the GLO 1865 surveys that instead of following the north fork of the North Fork of the American River, the trail, or a branch of it, turned northwest out of Six Mile Valley to the top of Yuba Gap, thence running parallel to and just south of I-80 to Carpenter Flat. George R. Stewart states that both routes were used.

Open, grassy Carpenter Flat was a stopping place along the trail before the hazardous descent over Emigrant Gap into Bear Valley. Because of the extensive road and railroad grading in the area there is no evidence of the trail from there to the top of Emigrant Gap.

The remaining stump of this tree bears scars from ropes used by emigrants to snub wagons down from Emigrant Gap.

There is about eighty feet of railroad fill in the gap itself. Looking down from the top of this gap, it is obvious that the only way for wagons to reach the valley was by going straight down a long, thirty-degree slide using whatever braking devices that could be devised. A switchback road now crosses this slide three times. Halfway down there is an old cedar stump which bears very definite deep scars around the circumference from snubbing ropes used by the emigrants. The course of the trail into Bear Valley is now crossed by Highway 20 near the present Bowman Lake Road turn-off.

John Steele's diary described the descent to Bear Valley in 1850: "All but one yoke of oxen were removed from each wagon, the wheels rough-locked, and a line tied to the hind axle by which three or four men held fast to regulate the motion. The wagons were then shoved off, when one after another thundered down over the rocks. through a cloud of dust, into the valley below."

After crossing the Bowman Lake Road in a northwesterly direction to the present PG&E group campground, and keeping on the south side of the valley, the trail again crosses Highway 20 just south of the bridge over Bear River. In this area, the only remaining evidence of the trail is found where it climbed over a low granite shoulder 200 yards west of the bridge. On this shoulder is a distinct eroded trail. Bear Valley, characterized by wet, swampy areas on both sides of the river, was mentioned in emigrant diaries as a resting place for people and animals.

These trail ruts can be seen passing through the center of Six Mile Valley.

The trail leading to Carpenter Flats runs along the North Fork of the North Fork of the American River.

The descent into Bear Valley from Emigrant Gap, as pictured here, proved to be a very difficult task. Railroad fill has covered most traces of the trail.

The author's dog, Oley, admires the view overlooking the Nevada City Cutoff.

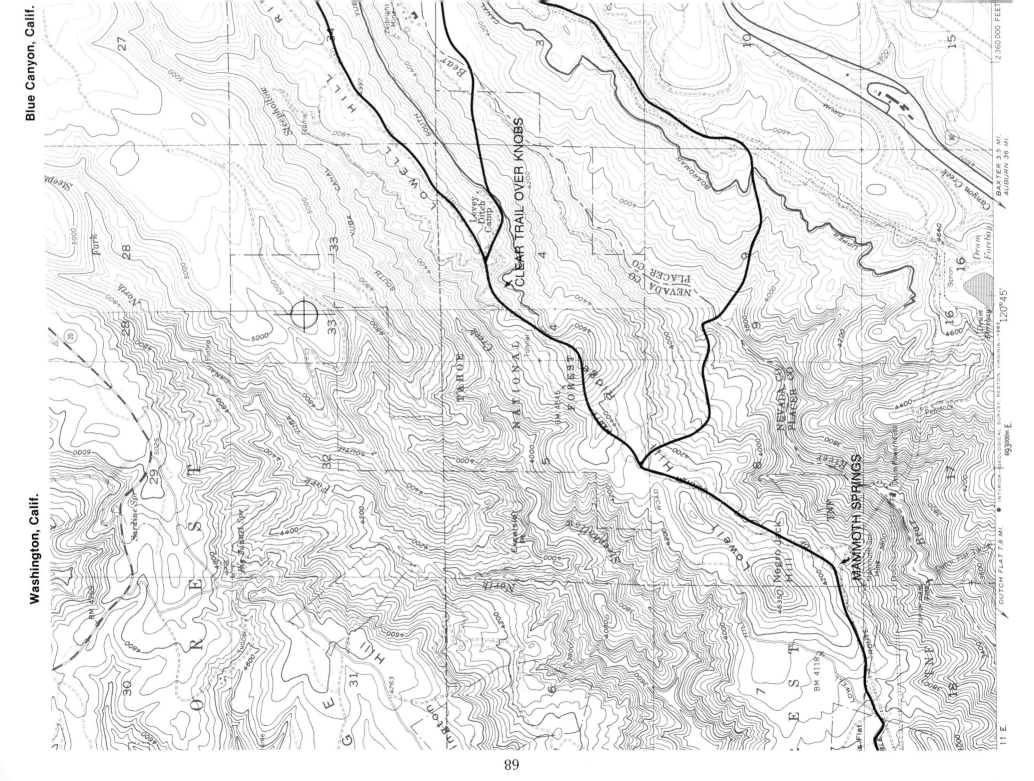

CLEAR TRAIL OVER KNOBS

MAMMOTH SPRINGS

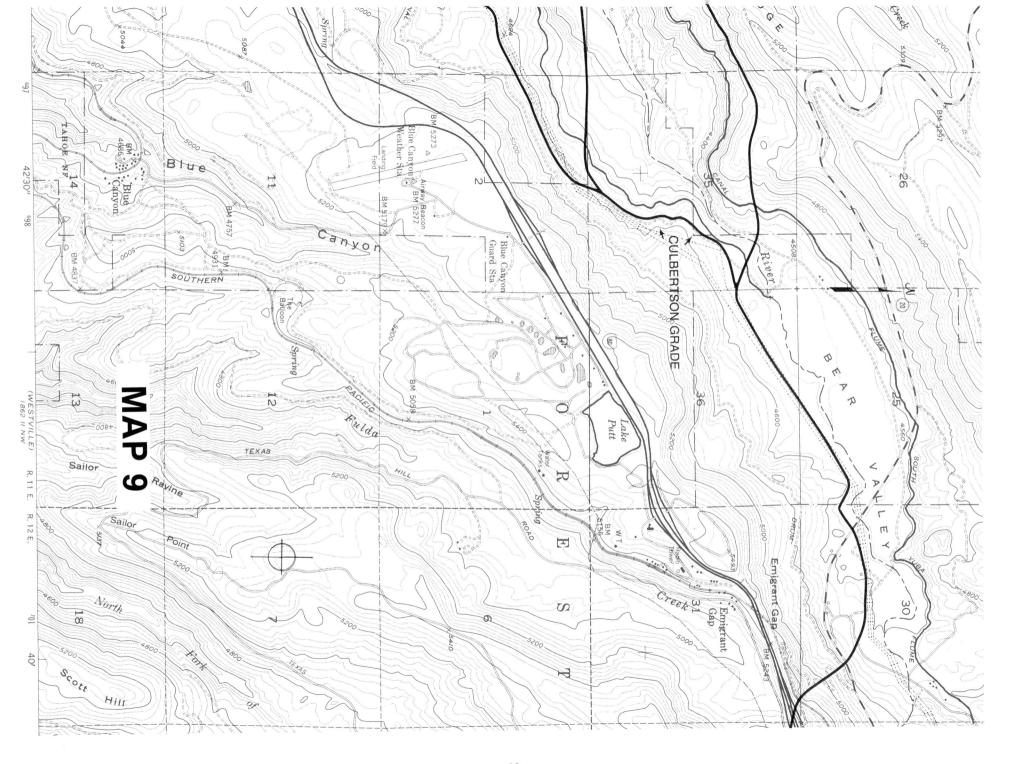

MAP 9

Map 9   Bear Valley to Mammoth Springs

TRAVELING SOUTHWEST, the trail left the open meadows of Bear Valley along the trace of the present power line and entered the timber. Within 300 yards it swung west off the power line and met the old Culbertson Grade, a former toll road. Between the power line and road, a short section of eroded old trail with faint rust marks on the granite has been located.

From that point on little evidence of the original trail on either side of Bear Valley can be found. The many roads and trails resulting from over 100 years of intensive mining and logging in the valley, plus rapid ground growth, landslides, and erosion, make it particularly difficult to find valid evidence here.

The steep canyon below the open valley soon forced the emigrants to ascend Lowell Hill Ridge to the north. After 1849 there were at least two routes out of the valley. In 1850 Micajah Littleton wrote: "For 2 miles after you leave Bear Valley you have the steepest hill and the longest one perhaps on the route one mile from where you came into the valley you come to the forks of the road one goes down to Steep Hollow (main trail) and the other by Nevada City when you take the right one you turn as though you were coming back." (Littleton's party went to Nevada City and Marysville on a route which State Highway 20 now generally follows.)

Local old-timers say that the trail crossed Bear River near Zeilbright Mine and reached the top of the ridge above Levy Ditch Camp. There is an excellent ford at Ziebright Mine, and faint traces of a road are seen near the top of the ridge. However, the two routes described below and shown on the map appear to be the ones most likely used. Perhaps there were others, but this writer will not vouch for them. It will be left to younger and more agile trail researchers to uncover evidence on the locations of the Bear River crossings.

In 1949 Bert Wiley, who compiled the state trail survey in 1939, mapped a route which forded the river one-quarter mile below the end of the open valley, climbed up and over a large granite outcrop, and traversed to the top of Lowell Hill Ridge at a saddle one mile

The trail crossed a series of steep knobs as it proceeded along the top of Lowell Hill Ridge.

southwest of present Highway 20. He later confirmed this route after a ground fire in 1954 had clearly exposed the wagon wheel tracks. By 1972 they had again disappeared because of erosion and deep humus.

This may have been the Nevada City cutoff, but it was probably also used to turn southwest down the ridge to the main trail, as is suggested by ruts seen on bare knobs just past Levy Ditch Camp. This long, narrow ridge is characterized by a series of steep hills and knobs along its top and by precipitous side slopes. In order to avoid the side slopes the trail kept to the very top of these hills.

Another crossing, marked by Robie's signs, appears at an excellent fording site approximately three miles below the open valley and ties in with what John Markle wrote on Aug. 27, 1849, after camping in the valley the night before: "For 5 miles the road was as usual rough and hilly. 3 miles brought us where we crossed the river and we then ascended 2 hills, the second so steep we had to double team." Edwin Bryant in 1847 and Wakeman Bryarly in 1849 also recorded that they proceeded some distance below the valley before ascending Lowell Hill. Robie stated that the trail followed a shelf above Culbertson Grade for two miles before dropping down to a ford. Unfortunately, this shelf is now practically obliterated by a power line, and the ford and trail down to it were destroyed by a landslide in 1986.

After a steep traverse up the side of Lowell Hill to a saddle just northeast of Negro Jack Hill, the trail turned southwest along the ridge. More research is needed to determine the precise trace of the ascent. From the ridge it followed close along a dirt road branching south off Lowell Hill Road at the northeast end of Negro Jack Hill. This road, soon brush-choked, continues straight ahead along the southeast shoulder of the hill, only to fork within 200 yards. The upper fork quickly breaks out of the brush, and the unimpeded trail, showing later use, continues on an easy, ungraded traverse around the south side of Negro Jack Hill.

One-quarter mile northeast of Mammoth Spring Mine on a brush-covered flat along the trail is said to be the location of John C. Fremont's flagpole, made from a stripped pine. Fremont camped in this area during his explorations in 1846. Mammoth Springs, above the mine and used by emigrants, is now dried up.

Bryant described the trip down the ridge this way: "In the afternoon we travelled along a high ridge sometimes over elevated peaks, with deep and frightful abysses yawning their darkened and hideous depths beneath us."

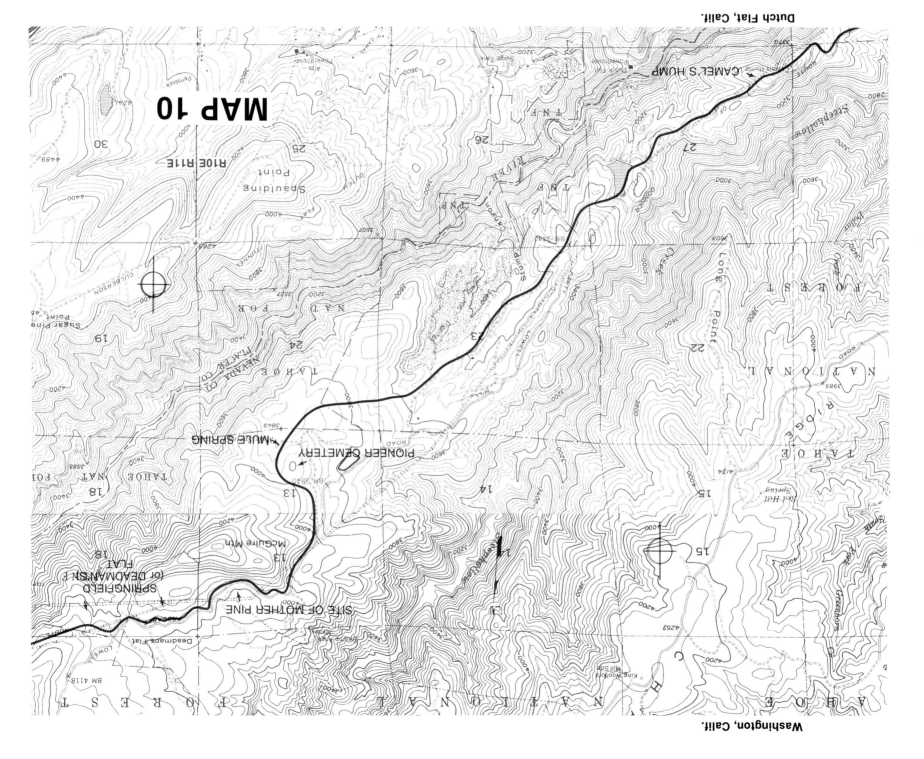

MAP 10

CAMEL'S HUMP

MULE SPRING

PIONEER CEMETERY

SITE OF MOTHER PINE

SPRINGFIELD
(or DEADMAN'S)
FLAT

Map 10 Springfield Flat to Camel's Hump

ONE-HALF MILE BEYOND Mammoth Springs the trail reached Springfield Flat (Deadman's Flat on the map) in the saddle between Negro Jack Hill and Maguire Mountain. Springfield Flat provided a grassy, waterfed meadow where many emigrants camped. From here the old trail closely followed Lowell Hill Road around the north side of Maguire Mountain. About one-half mile beyond Springfield Flat the trail passed the "Mother Pine," made famous in emigrant diaries because of its unusually large size. This tree stood on a flat area on the right side of Lowell Hill Road.

The trail continued along the trace of Lowell Hill Road around the western shoulder of Maguire Mountain and soon turned south close along the dirt road which leaves Lowell Hill Road in the NE¼ SW¼ Section 13. Recent logging has obliterated any remaining trace of the trail in the Mule Springs area. One of Robie's few remaining signs was found in the draw just north of a round, wooded knob 300 yards northwest of Mule Springs. A very old, small, unmarked cemetery sometimes referred to as "Pioneer Graveyard" is located on top of this knob. Mule Spring lies at the head of a small meadow. It is marked with a Forest Service sign indicating that because of the deep snow, one of the Donner relief parties left its mules here and continued eastward on foot, packing their supplies on their backs. After tracing the tortuous trail from Donner Lake, it is hard to realize how these relief parties got through during the heavy snows of 1846-47.

Intensive logging and mining for gold below Mule Spring over a period of many years have eliminated the possibility of tracking the trail for the next two miles. Both Robie and Wiley indicated that it generally followed the Mule Spring drainage to Liberty Hill Diggings, entered and followed Stump Canyon for a short distance, then turned right up to the present Lowell Hill Ridge, deviating from the present road only to avoid steep side grades by going over the top of several hills and knobs, including steep and precarious Camel's Hump. This landmark, which is on the boundary of the Tahoe National Forest, was used as the western terminus of this survey.

Beginning in 1849 many emigrants broke off their trip and joined the gold seekers in the "diggins" along Lowell Hill Ridge and farther west.

Bryarly, in his diary entry of August 30, 1849, mentions his first sight of the gold "diggins" along here and also describes the conditions of his party as it neared the end of the long journey. "Our teams are now so weak that they can scarcely pull up the slightest hill. We came upon a creek along which they were digging. One large washer got out one pound in two hours. The teams were so far given out that we decided to leave half of the wagons and take half on with the mules. The principal reason for haste is the melancholy fact that we had not provisions enough to last three days. Our meat had been out for ten days. Bread and coffee was all we had. Oak leaves was our only provender for our already broken down mules." Other diaries indicate that the condition of Bryarly's party was typical of the emigrant wagon trains that successfully crossed the mighty Sierra Nevada.

At the end of Lowell Hill Ridge the emigrants crossed the last obstacle of Steep Hollow Creek. Issac Wistar describes the party's descent into Steep Hollow in 1849:

> August 25th. Being delayed by hunting for stray mules, this morning we got off late and were brought up at the brink of a long, precipitous descent which at first seemed like an effectual bar for wagons in that direction. Nevertheless, it was the termination of a long leading ridge the whole of which would have to be retraced to search for a more practicable descent; so we determined to try it and went to work. Commencing with my Cincinnati wagon, which is the smallest and best, we chained the wheels, took out the four lead mules, leaving only the wheelers, cut and chained to the rear axle as large a tree as we could handle for a drag, put all hands on the back ropes, and lowered away. The descent was two miles long, with some bad turns and "jump-offs," but it was at length thus successfully accomplished with both wagons. In climbing up again to get the loose stock, I hastily pulled my rifle

out of a bush where I had concealed it about half-way up, when it discharged itself in my face, the ball piercing my hat in three places, giving my hair a smart wrench and scorching both hairs and eyebrows.

From Steep Hollow the trail broke out into the rolling Sierra foothills and generally followed Bear River to the lush Sacramento Valley at Johnson's Ranch, near present-day Wheatland, where their terrible ordeal ended.

TAHOE *National Forest*

DONNER LAKE

MULE SPRING

WATERING AND RESTING POINT ON DONNER TRAIL
THIS WAS THE FURTHEST POINT TO WHICH PACK
ANIMALS COULD TRAVEL IN BRINGING FOOD TO
THE STRANDED DONNER PARTY IN THE WINTER OF
1846 – 47 FROM HERE THE RESCUE PARTIES
CARRIED 50 POUND PACKS THROUGH DEEP SNOW T

Emigrants stopped for water at Mule Spring on Lowell Hill Ridge.

Easy-to-Reach
Points of Interest

MOST OF THE POINTS listed below can be easily reached by car. Page numbers direct the reader to descriptions of each location.

1. **DOG VALLEY** (page 22). Take I-80 to the Verdi offramp and proceed to the center of the Verdi business section. Turn northwest at Dog Valley Road (Bridge St.) Cross the Truckee River and drive past the old Crystal Peak Cemetery. Continue up Dog Valley Road for three miles. Dog Valley is directly ahead, where the road turns sharply to the southwest around Crystal Peak.

2. **SECOND SUMMIT** (page 22). Continue southwest from Dog Valley two and one-half miles to the Tahoe National Forest entrance sign.

3. **GEORGE & JACOB DONNER CAMP, 1846-47** (page 34). Turn north onto State Highway 89 from the I-80 offramp one mile east of Truckee. Proceed north for two and one-half miles to the Donner Camp picnic area, which is close to the highway.

4. **DONNER MEMORIAL PARK** (page 34). Turn south at the I-80 offramp one-quarter mile west of the Truckee Agricultural Inspection Station. The park entrance is adjacent to the highway.

5. **ENTRANCE TO COLD STREAM CANYON** (page 42). Take the same offramp as above. Drive south past the park, a service station, a restaurant, and a gravel plant. The entrance to the valley is less than one mile south of I-80.

6. **"CHINESE WALL" IN DONNER PASS** (page 40). From the same offramp turn west along Donner Pass Road (old Highway 40), which runs along the north side of Donner Lake and winds up to the original Donner Pass. Stop on the last turn before reaching the observation point on the old highway. The stone retaining wall, built by Chinese railroad workers to support the SPRR tracks, blocks the final gap used by the emigrants to reach the summit. It can be easily seen from the highway.

7. **DONNER PASS SUMMIT** (page 39). Continue west up Donner Pass Road to the very summit. Turn south on a secondary road for about 300 yards. At a dirt road turn left and continue for seventy-five yards. An emigrant trail sign marks the top of the pass in a narrrow draw.

8. **ROLLER PASS** (page 46). The well-marked trailhead of the Pacific Crest Trail is found alongside the emigrant trail marker at the top of old Donner Pass (see 7 above). Walk south on the trail for two miles as it traverses up the west side of Mount Judah. The top of Roller Pass is at the lowest point in a saddle between Mount Judah and Mount Lincoln. Turn left off the trail and proceed for one hundred yards to a U.S. Forest Service sign which marks the lip of the pass.

9. **SUMMIT VALLEY** (page 49). Take the Soda Springs offramp from I-80 and drive east through Soda Springs on old Highway 40. One mile beyond Soda Springs the valley can be seen from the road.

10. **TRAIL BEHIND BIG BEND RANGER STATION** (page 58). Take the Rainbow Road offramp from I-80 and turn south. Drive one mile west on old Highway 40, passing Rainbow Tavern, to a widened gravel area just below an oblong granite knob on the north side of the road. The old trail can be seen going along the north side of this knob in a southwesterly direction. Numerous rust-stained rocks and trees scarred by wagon wheel hubs can be found here.

11. **SIX-MILE VALLEY** (page 64). Take the Yuba Gap offramp from I-80 and drive south for about one mile on the road to Lake Valley Reservoir. The beautiful valley can be seen on the left, a short distance before coming to the Eagle Mountain Ski Lodge.

12. **EMIGRANT GAP** (page 64). Take the Emigrant Gap offramp from I-80 and take a steep gravel road leading north up to the S.P.R.R. tracks. Walk directly across the tracks and look down the steep dropoff used by the emigrants to reach Bear Valley. This gap is about one-half mile east of the Emigrant Gap observation area.

13. **BEAR VALLEY** (page 64). Bear Valley can be reached in either direction on State Highway 20 four miles west of its turnoff from I-80. An emigrant trail sign on the south side of the Highway 20 bridge over Bear River indicates where the trail went down the south side of the river. Two hundred yards west of the highway the trail can be easily picked up going over a granite shoulder.

14. **MULE SPRING** (page 73). Twenty-three miles east of Nevada City on Highway 20, turn south onto Lowell Hill Ridge Road, which is at the top of the grade coming west up out of Bear Valley. Drive seven miles south on Lowell Hill Ridge Road to a dirt road to the left marked by a sign pointing to Mule Spring. Drive in about one half mile and park. Mule Spring, marked by a U.S. Forest Service sign, is reached by walking about 250 yards to the east on an old road that has been blocked to vehicular traffic. (Of additional interest: two miles south of Highway 20 along the side of Lowell Hill Ridge Road, two bald knobs showing the original trail can be seen crossing the very top of the narrow ridge.)

References

1. California Legislature. *Assembly Daily Journal,* January 21, 1949. Consideration of House Resolution No. 52, Report on Overland Emigrant Trail.
2. Curran, Harold. *Fearful Crossing.* Great Basin Press, Reno, 1982.
3. Daigle, Russell D. "Report on Ride over the Old Donner Emigrant Trail Between Bear Valley and Steephollow." August 1940.   Copy in S.O., Tahoe National Forest.
4. Division of Beaches and Parks, State of California.
   a. "Report on Overland Emigrant Trail," Dec. 1, 1949. California State Office of Historic Preservation.
   b. "Plan of Proposed Overland Emigrant Trail State Historical Monument," (Survey Maps) 1950. Office of Central Records, Parks and Recreation, Sacramento.
5. General Land Office. 1866 Survey Maps of T17N R15E, T17N R14E, T17n R13E, T17n R12E, MDM. Copies in S.O., Tahoe National Forest.
6. Harris, E. W. "The Early Emigrant Pass Between Mt. Judah and Mt. Lincoln." *Nevada Historical Society Quarterly,* Spring 1979.
7. Hermann, Ruth. *The Paiutes of Pyramid Lake,* Harlan-Young Press: San Jose, 1972.
8. Hunt, Tom. *Ghost Trails to California,* American West Publishing Co.: Palo Alto, 1974.
9. Jefferson, T. H. "Map of the Emigrant Road — Independence, Missouri to San Francisco, California," 1849.
10. Morgan, Dale. *Overland in 1846 — Diaries and Letters of the California Oregon Trail.* Talisman Press: Georgetown, Calif., 1963.
11. Nevada Historical Society. *The Overland Emigrant Trail to California A Guide.* Nevada Emigrant Trail Marking Committee: Reno, 1975.
12. Rhoads, Earl. "Maps of Emigrant Trail, Verdi, Nevada to Summit Valley, Cal., as marked and traced by P.M. Weddell of San Jose, 1920-1952." In possession of Dan Rhoads, Monterey, Calif.
13. Robie, Wendell T. "A Centennial Year Proposal Concerning the Old Emigrant Road." May 28, 1935. Searls Historical Library, Nevada City, Calif.
14. Stewart, George R. *The California Trail.* McGraw-Hill: New York, 1962.
    _____ *Donner Pass.* Lane Books: Menlo Park, 1964.
    _____ *The Opening of the California Trail.* University of California Press, 1953.
15. Street, Franklin. *California in 1850 — A Concise Description of the Overland Route from the Missouri River by the South Pass to Sacramento City.* R. E. Edwards & Co.: Cincinnati, 1851.
16. Wiley, Bert. *The Overland Emigrant Trail in California.* Sacramento, 1982.
17. Weddell, Peter M. "Map of Historic Emigrant Trail." Seals Historical Library, Nevada City. Location of Donner Camps & Marking Trail. The Pony Express. Placerville, 1949.

Other Western Books Published
or Marketed by The Patrice Press

These books may be purchased from your local bookseller or by direct mail order from

The Patrice Press
1701 South Eighth St.
St. Louis MO 63104

There is a $2 shipping and handling charge for the first book and 75 cent charge for each additional book.
You may call toll-free at **1-800-367-9242** to place your order.

The Oregon Trail Revisited, by Gregory M. Franzwa. 419 pages. Cloth, $14.95, ISBN 0-935284-57-5; paper, $7.95, ISBN 0-935284-58-3

Historic Sites Along the Oregon Trail, by Aubrey L. Haines. 439 pages. Cloth, $24.95; paper, $12.95, ISBN 0-935284-21-4.

Maps of the Oregon Trail, by Gregory M. Franzwa. 292 pages. Cloth, $24.95, ISBN 0-935284-30-3; paper, $14.95, ISBN 0-935284-32-X; looseleaf, $27.95, ISBN 0-935284-31-1.

The Wake of the Prairie Schooner, by Irene D. Paden. 514 pages. Cloth, $24.95, ISBN 0-935284-40-0; paper, $12.95, ISBN 0-935284-38-9.

To the Land of Gold and Wickedness: The 1848-1859 Diary of Lorena Hays, Jeanne Watson, ed. 496 pages. Cloth, $27.95, ISBN 0-935284-53-2.

The Latter-day Saints' Emigrants' Guide, by Wm. Clayton; Stanley B. Kimball, Ph.D., ed. 107 pages. Paper, $9.95, ISBN 0-935284-27-3.

Platte River Road Narratives, by Merrill J. Mattes. 672 pages, 8½″ x 11″. Cloth, $95.

The Great Platte River Road, by Merrill J. Mattes. 583 pages. Cloth, $36.95; paper, $16.95.

Following the Santa Fe Trail, by Marc Simmons, Ph.D. 214 pages. Paper, $12.95.

Ghost Trails to California, by Tom Hunt. 288 pages, 8½″ x 11″. Cloth, $34.95; paper, $22.95.

Fearful Crossing: The Central Overland Trail Through Nevada, by Harold Curran. 212 pages. Paper, $14.95.

Forty-niners, by Archer Butler Hulbert. 340 pages. Paper, $14.95.

Exploring the American West, 1803-1879, by William Goetzmann. 128 pages. Paper, $7.95.

Indian, Soldier, and Settler, by Robert M. Utley. 84 pages. $8.95.

The Overland Migrations, by David Lavender. 111 pages. $7.95.

Fort Laramie, by David Lavender. 159 pages. Paper, $8.95.

Fort Vancouver, by David Lavender. 143 pages. Paper, $8.95.

Whitman Mission, by Erwin N. Thompson. 92 pages. Paper, $4.45.

Scotts Bluff, by Merrill J. Mattes. 64 pages. Paper, $2.45.